Wilshamstead
Homestead of Friends

Wilshamstead

Homestead of Friends

Christine Papworth
Gessie Della Ripa

Published by

Matador
12 Manor Walk, Coventry Road
Market Harborough
Leics LE16 9BP, UK
Tel: (+44) 1858 468828 / 469898
Fax: (+44) 1858 431649
Email: matador@troubador.co.uk
Web: www.troubador.co.uk/matador

ISBN 1 899293 03 5

Cover: Design by Barry Huckle
(Front: top left, wheelwrights; bottom left, bake house Church Road; top right, Elephant and Castle Public House; Church House; Dane Oak; bottom right, Millennium village sign
(Back: top, All Saints Church; cottage in Church Road; bottom, Little Church Farm

The publisher makes no representation, express or implied, with regard to the accuracy of the information contained in this book and cannot accept any legal responsibility or liability for any errors or omissions that may be made.

Every effort has been made to trace the holders of copyright materials used in this publication. Should any omissions become apparent, the publishers will be happy to make the necessary arrangements at the first opportunity.

Typesetting: Troubador Publishing Ltd, Market Harborough, UK
Printed and bound by Cambrian Printers, Aberystwyth, Wales

Matador is an imprint of Troubador Publishing Ltd

CONTENTS

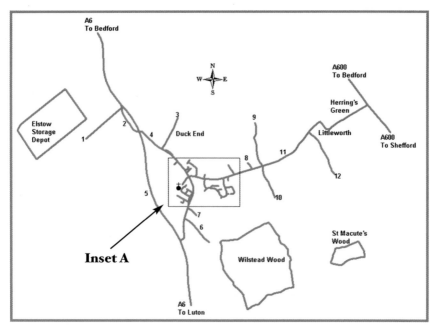

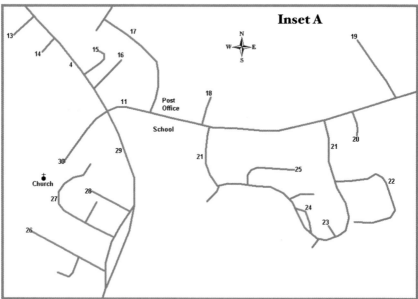

1	Dane Lane	11	Cotton End Road	21	Whitworth Way
2	Bedford Road Loop	12	Elms Lane	22	Armstrong Close
3	Duck End Lane	13	The Square	23	Morgan Close
4	Bedford Road	14	Black Hat Close	24	Phipps Close
5	A6 Wilstead Bypass	15	Bird Court	25	Hampton Close
6	Briar Bank Mobile Home Park	16	Town Close	26	Vicarage Lane
7	Howard Close	17	Dines Close	27	Pollards Close
8	Northwood Lane	18	Castle Close	28	Home Close
9	Hooked Lane	19	Northwood Lane	29	Luton Road
10	Ivy Lane	20	Brambles	30	Church Road

FOREWORD

To record 10,000 years of the story of a Bedfordshire village is a notable achievement and the authors are to be congratulated on their painstaking research into the history of Wilshamstead.

The village is typical of all that is best in so many Bedfordshire villages. As the authors point out in their introduction "....very few gentry and professional classes resided here". And yet for 10,000 years Wilshamstead families have brought up their young, have tilled their fields, looked after their livestock, built and repaired their schools and places of worship, provided the inhabitants with shops and inns and generally gone about their business peacefully and without fuss. They are the real heroes and heroines of this book. True, Wilshamstead has had its share of villains over the years, but no more so than neighbouring villages.

I hope that present and future generations of Wilstonians will enjoy reading this book and learn to honour those who trod the lanes and fields of their village in past generations as well as looking to the future as Wilshamstead enters its next millennium.

Sam Whitbread
June 2002

INTRODUCTION

Wilshamstead with its hamlets of Littleworth and Duck End is an ancient parish. In existence before the Domesday Book of 1086, it has always been an open parish which supported a variety of trades and services of the lower classes. Despite having two Lords of the Manor, very few gentry and professional classes resided here.

The original nucleus is likely to have existed around a large green to the south east of the church, centred on what today is the crossroads. Gradually several homesteads established along the roadway which would eventually become Cotton End Road.

By the 17th century, these early pockets of occupation had formed a number of small 'ends' latterly named for example, Chapel End and Potters End. As the population grew, the gaps between the houses slowly filled in.

The gradual expansion continued to follow the line of the main roadway, which connected the two larger roads at each end of the parish, thus giving the strung

Wilshamstead in the 1960s

(Reproduced with the kind permission of Enid Wisson)

out appearance for which the parish is known. In 1671, the population was 387 and by the turn of the 21st century it had risen to around 2400 people.

Another example of historical influence on the shape of the parish is the northern boundary. Characterised by right angle turns, it is believed to have been fixed after the ground was already cultivated in furlongs.

The formal parish boundary does not include the hamlet of Herring's Green to the east of the parish but there is evidence that this tiny hamlet, which clustered around a green long gone, played its part. One instance is the popular belief that Johanne Heroun listed in the 14th century Wilshamstead subsidy rolls may have lived there and the area became known by this personal name.

So formed and defined by its own history, the parish lies at the base of the Greensand Ridge, 4 miles south of the county town of Bedford.

The authors hope you enjoy this book and its mix of local, social and family history that occurred within this area of England that has been defined as Wilshamstead.

CHAPTER 1

Wil's Homestead: The First Millennium

In this first part of the history of the village we will travel through a broad band of more than 1,000 years from the Stone Age to the Invaders.

There are no written records for early history and so we must rely on archaeological evidence to point to people living in the parish. The first confirmation of occupation of Wilshamstead begins in the Mesolithic or Middle Stone Age period which started about 8,000 BC, when the population of Britain is estimated to have been less than one million people. A stone tranchet axe dating from this period was discovered in St Macute's Wood. Hand axes were primarily used for butchery but were probably used for a number of other purposes. This axe is now on display in Bedford Museum.

Occupation continued on into the New Stone Age period around 4,000 BC with a Neolithic axe being found in Wilstead Wood. Farming started during this period and this included the clearance of trees. This would have been on a very small scale but it is possible to imagine the axe being used in the wood. The creation of these axes was time consuming but once completed they were hafted or bound to a wooden handle with plant fibres, animal guts or leather thongs. Unfortunately although an authenticated archaeological find, the Neolithic axe was only shown to the museum for verification by a private individual and so it can not be viewed.

Other flint artefacts from the Stone Age have been discovered in the recent archaeological dig on the site of the new Oakley Grange development and a hard hammer flake in fields to the south of Elstow storage depot.

Moving into the Bronze Age which began about 2000 BC, we know people were living in the village because a number of objects were discovered and recorded in the vicinity of the open fields to the north of the parish. These documented items, together with catalogued marks in the landscape, are estimated to date from this period, showing settlement took place at this time.

2001 Archaeological excavation at Oakley grange site

The population of the parish continued to grow and by the Iron Age (750 BC – 43 AD) there were a number of areas of settlement. The Catuvellauni tribe were the native people occupying the area. In 2001, Iron Age settlements were excavated in the large fields behind Church Farm and Little Church Farm prior to the new housing development of Oakley Grange. This was the first official archaeological dig carried out in the parish of Wilstead. This archaeological dig uncovered a small farmstead from the early Iron Age, approximately 2500 years ago, and it has been presumed to have been occupied by a single family. The animal bones and burnt seeds that were recovered showed that mixed agriculture was being practised. There was no evidence that the farmstead was protected by field ditches, suggesting the landscape was quite open.

It is thought the ridge in this vicinity is likely to have been an Iron Age boundary.

An enclosed Iron Age site also occurs in the fields to the north of the parish in the vicinity of the Bronze Age site previously found. Consisting of rectilinear and circular enclosures and a pit, the settlement site yielded a late Iron Age pottery vessel indicating probable continuous occupation of this site throughout the Iron Age.

On the other side of the parish in fields near Hammer Hill, shards of Belgic pottery also from the late Iron Age were reported in 1980.

By the time of the Roman Conquest in 43 AD the Catuvellauni people in our parish were open to new ideas. Becoming a pro-Roman people they quickly adopted Roman lifestyles and Roman rule. A transitional settlement showing the gradual move to becoming Romano British was discovered in the Oakley Grange dig. A new farmstead in a different location to that of the Iron Age farm commenced approximately 50 years before the Roman invasion. This site showed the inhabitants living and working within a regular layout of fields and enclosures. This time, the farmstead was protected by ditches.

Marks within soil indicate occupation

The foundations of two timber buildings were located along with a number of iron nails and it is also thought that a stone building existed as Roman roof tiles were discovered in the vicinity. Unearthed animal bones and charred seeds show that these Romano–British Wilstead farmers had sheep and cows and were growing spelt wheat. Further support for this was evident in the discovery of an iron wool comb used in sheep farming and a Roman quern stone for grinding wheat.

The discovery of three deliberately placed sheep skulls from a variety of horn-less sheep common to later Roman Britain indicates animal sacrifice occurring at this farmstead. The skulls were placed within a small pit all facing different directions. It is thought two other skulls were also present but this is subject to the analysis which is taking place at the time of writing.

Everyday life continued throughout the early Roman period with huge quantities of pottery, personal bronze cleaning items, bronze coins and an iron ring being discovered at this farmstead. Iron hobnails from Roman shoes were excavated and also a large Roman water pit. The pottery was mainly locally produced but some Samian Ware was imported from France showing that trading was taking place. The farmstead seems to have been abandoned in the later Roman period and the people moved away.

The excavations also turned up some remains of early Wilstonians. Two deposits within 5 metres of each other contained fragments of bone. One pit held 4 finger bones, the other 26 skull fragments. It was the Roman practice to have burial grounds away from the living areas so these deposits were either the continuation by the inhabitants of the pre-Roman practice of excarnation (leaving human bodies exposed to the elements to enable the soul to be freed by natural processes) or their farming activity had disturbed earlier burials.

Another site of early occupation is located in the fields to the south of Elstow storage depot. Two sites of enclosed settlements have been investigated just off the crest of the hill known locally as The Knoll. One enclosure dates from the late

*Roman storage jar at the
Oakley Grange Development
archaeological excavation*

Iron Age/ Roman conquest period whilst the other is of 1st century AD. These
enclosures are rare as most settlements of these periods are found in gravel valleys
and this one is on the Oxford Clay. The predominance of pottery found came from
domestic cooking and storage vessels made of locally produced greyware and shelly
ware. However, fragments of Verulamium White Ware and Samian Ware, both
coming from Lezoux in Central Gaul, France were also found.

Returning to our settlement in the open fields to the north of the parish, we
have evidence that occupation carried on into the middle Roman British period.

A report of kiln bars and wasters suggest that a pottery kiln site was at
Littleworth and coins from the reigns of Septimius Severus (193 – 211 AD) and
Gallienus (253 –268 AD) were found in this area.

A later Roman British Site is located nearby in the fields of Village Farm currently farmed by the Crouch family. A metal fibula brooch from the 2nd – 3rd century AD was found. These brooches were worn as a decorative safety pin. Coins
were also located from the reign of Constantius II (337 – 361 AD) and Valentinian
I (364 – 375 AD) and these confirm occupation into the 4th century AD.

A wide scatter of Roman British pottery including some Samian pottery has
been discovered in all of these fields in the north of the parish. The aerial photograph on page 5 shows marks in the crops indicating one location of settlement in
the north of the parish.

We should not leave the Roman period however without paying note to the local
legend that says a Roman Road runs along the east parish boundary near to the
A600 road from Shefford. Although a number of theories have been documented
on this idea, there is to date, no official definitive agreement to this suggestion.
Similarly though, no full investigation has ever been carried out to disprove the
idea.

In the early 5th century the Roman rulers left Britain and our villagers were open
to the influences of new invaders. Approximately, from around 500 AD until the

turn of the millennium in 1000 AD, these Invaders included Angles, Saxons, Jutes and Danes.

A lasting reminder of the Anglo-Saxon government is the name of the locality within which the parish falls. A Hundred was the legal and tax gathering Anglo Saxon area that comprised of 100 hides of ground. Each hide was the amount of land (normally around 120 acres) that would support a family and its dependants. Wilshamstead villagers fell into the Redbornstoke Hundred and this name is still with us today although its significance has disappeared.

The most poignant reminder for the village of the Anglo-Saxons influence is the name of the village. Wil's Homestead is a corruption of the Anglo–Saxon name of Winessamsted. A full explanation of this is given in the Name Game chapter in this book.

The cap (top) of a skull of a 9th century Anglo Saxon villager was discovered in the grounds of the current vicarage in 1997. Following authentication it has now been reburied in the churchyard. It is likely that this cap was removed from the rest of the skull by ploughing when the trees were planted many years before. The vicarage was probably a religious site or a burial ground in pre-Christian times. Small slithers of stone apparently dating from pre Christian period have also been found on the vicarage grounds.

A local legend suggests a camp of the invading Danes was located in the vicinity of Dane Farm and Dane Lane to the west of the parish. To date however this can not be supported by any documentary or archaeological evidence as little investigation has been undertaken in this area.

As the first millennium closed our villagers had travelled from primitive Stone Age to a people facing the imminent conquest by the Normans from France in 1066.

CHAPTER 2

Our People,
Our Heritage

A number of village sons have risen to prominence or fame over the years and in these pages we shall meet them.

Probably the most famous was **Sir William Morgan**. Any trip to the churchyard of All Saints would not be complete without a visit to his tomb. Its richly engraved marble top reflects the accomplishments of the successful politician he came to be. Born in 1829, William left the village at the age of 19 for the shores of Australia in the company of two brothers and a sister. When he arrived in Australia he worked for a short time in the Australian outback before becoming a grocers assistant for Messrs Boord in Adelaide.

Sir William Morgan

(Reproduced with kind permission of the Speaker of the House of Assembly, South Australia)

Succumbing to the temptation of the Victoria gold rush in 1851, William and his brother Thomas went to the Bendigo gold diggings. Being more successful than most they made their fortunes and William returned to Adelaide, promptly buying out the Boord Brothers business. In 1854 he married Harriet and together they raised 5 children. Over a period of time, Morgan & Co was expanded and improved until it became one of the leading mercantile houses in the colony. From this success, William helped to found the Bank of Adelaide in 1865. As one of the wealthiest men in the colony, William entered into politics. In 1871 he was elected to the legislative council and after enduring a stormy political career he rose to the prestigious office of Premier of

> **DID YOU KNOW?**
>
> John Bunyan's ancestor William Bunion was farming at Wilstead in 1199

South Australia on September 27 1878.

During his time in office he was responsible for extensive public works including the start of the national gallery, the first parts of the Adelaide University and the first deep drainage system for an Australian city.

Although his shrewdness and foresight brought him to the front of politics his own business life was beset by pressures. In addition to his other interests William had bought a share in the Balade Mines in New Caledonia which brought additional troubles. Eventually these pressures caused him to retire from the office of Premier on June 23 1881.

With his health affected by his troubles, William Morgan left for a short visit to England to try to recuperate. Leaving Australia in May 1883 he was created Knight Commander of the most distinguished order of St Michael and St George (K.C.M.G) upon arrival in England for his services overseas.

During that summer he visited his old home of Wilshamstead but illness prevented his expected return at Harvest Festival. Although not in attendance his generosity to the poor of the village at this time was noteworthy. Local folklore says that he died in the village and his ghost has been seen near the crossroads, outside the Manor House where the Morgan family once lived. In truth he died in November 1883 at Brighton, Sussex and was returned to Wilshamstead for burial. The whole village met the body, with the vicar and surpliced choir escorting the procession from the crossroads. The opening of the burial service took place at the church gates before proceeding into a full church.

One of our earliest prominent sons was the academic and cleric **William Samuel Richardson**. He was born in the Wilstead vicarage on 23 July 1698, the son of the vicar, Samuel Richardson. Educated at Oakham and Westminster he went to Emmanuel College Cambridge in 1715 to undertake scholarly work. It was at this college he was to make his name. He graduated as a bachelor of arts in 1719, a master of arts in 1723 and a doctor of divinity in 1735. During this period he was also ordained as a deacon in 1720 and a priest in 1722.

Although never a fellow of Emmanuel College, his close acquaintance with the

Portrait of William Samuel Richardson

*(Reproduced with kind permission of
The Master and Fellows of
Emmanuel College, Cambridge)*

fellows led to him unanimously and without his knowledge being elected to the position of master in 1736. He was known to be a strict disciplinarian and also a strong Tory in politics.

Whilst holding the post of college bursar for 38 years he is remembered for over-hauling the room rental system for students. He became involved in the remodel-ling of the college buildings but his architectural aspiration exceeded the funds raised and it is reported that the college was left in debt. His personal interest in history led him to establish a full list of masters since the college's formation and a number of other works which the college used as a reference basis. On two occa-sions William was also elected to the position of vice chancellor of the university.

Amongst his numerous posts he was also one of the King's chaplains from 1746 until 1768, after which time he undertook the precentorship at Lincoln. A precen-tor leads the congregation in singing and is responsible for the musical life of the cathedral.

Despite all of these roles and positions William Samuel Richardson is mostly remembered for his revision of Godwin's work 'De Praesulibus Angliae Commantarri'. This hugely important English episcopate work was designed to establish the precise episcopal succession of the English bishops and included many biographical details. Hailed as the finest book then issued by Cambridge Press it was published in 1743.

William Hale White is nationally known under his pen name of Mark Rutherford but it is a little known fact that the author is of Wilshamstead descent. Although he was born in Bedford, his ancestors both lived and were buried in the village. In his Groombridge diary he writes to his second wife: 'I have been told they lie buried in Wilshamstead churchyard. Wilshamstead is a small remote agri-cultural village in Bedfordshire. They were Bedfordshire folk and Bedfordshire was the HQ of puritan and cromwellian independency. My grandfather had his windows smashed by an angry Tory mob during the Napoleonic wars because he refused to illuminate for British Victories and my father also had his window destroyed because he was a member of Lord John Russell's committee at the borough elec-tion during the time of the reform bill. I seem to come of an honest set but social-ly nothing much above farmers who may have been and indeed likely were, officers in Oliver's Army'.

> **DID YOU KNOW?**
> At the start of World War 1, local family member, Wesley George Sharpe fitted the Duke of Gloucester, the Duke of Kent and the Queens father, the then Duke of York, with bicycles for their stay in Bedfordshire.

From author to artist we come to **Joseph Carrier** who was born in Biddenham in 1850. Although not a native of the village he was the master of the Wilstead national school from 1873 until 1882. He married in Biddenham, but his first four children were all baptised at All Saints, Wilshamstead. Carrier only had one arm, having lost one as a child in a field keeping accident whilst scaring rooks. People remembered him as a teacher and in 1941, Mr Boston who was residing in Bedford told the Bedfordshire Times how he recalled being taught by Carrier whilst at the Wilshamstead School. As a portrait artist, it is believed Carrier painted one of Lord Halsbury when he was Lord Chancellor, and he also exhibited at the Royal Academy. Her Grace, the Duchess of Bedford at that time also patronised his art by buying his work. After leaving Wilstead, he moved to Bromham free school before emigrating to Canada.

Farming has always been part of Wilstead life but one farming family changed the face of agriculture on a national scale. During the 19th century farmers were looking for improved methods and tools. The **Armstrongs**, farmers at Manor Farm and Vicarage Farm, were no exception. Creating an improved iron wheel plough they approached the local blacksmith to execute the implement to their specification. Its revolutionary design was soon recognised by John Howard, the Bedford foundry owner. Having larger production and marketing capabilities, Howard exhibited the new plough at the first ever Royal Agricultural show in 1839. The implement became known as the champion plough of England and was widely produced and exported from Howard's Brittania works, making him a small fortune.

'A plough of small size, with a mould board or furrow-turner of excellent form, calculated to give least resistance in turning over the furrow'
1839 Royal Agricultural Show

Photographed at Ramsey Rural Museum 2001

Nearly thirty years after its first showing the plough was again celebrated, this time at the 1868 show in Newcastle being described as the best general plough available. It was the forerunner of the present form of the English plough and its success was recorded in a contemporary poem. The poem also attributes other implement improvements to the Armstrong family although these designs did not reach the same level of fame.

> Still palm bedecks that plough
> Of Armstrongs made by Howard now
> Remitting by one third the toil
> While other ploughs take horses three
> Two draw the champion easily
> And other honours yet belong
> Unto the genius of Armstrong
> When you commit the seed to the ground
> The Zig Zag harrows best are found
> Twas he conceived the happy knack

No tine to trace another track
A third good honour, too he won
At harvest when the crop of grain
Is carried off, some will remain
This with the fork you cannot take
But can by using Armstrong's rake

W Franklyn 'The Plough' 1857

DID YOU KNOW?

Victor Wisson was a local councillor for around 40 years and became Mayor of Bedford in 1981 with the ceremony taking place at All Saints church.

(Reproduced with the kind permission of Dorothy Cooper)

CHAPTER 3

All Saints' Church

Almost hidden from the centre of the village stands the beautiful medieval parish church of All Saints. It was the first church in the village and its first centre of Christianity, where Wilshamtead's friendly spirit was first born. It was so called because a church is dedicated to a saint whose feast day falls closest to the date of the dedication. The church has not been built on a true east-west axis, which seems to suggest that the church may have been on an earlier site of worship.

Although the oldest remaining parts date from the English Gothic architecture of the 14th and 15th Centuries its origins are much older. Earliest records from the 13th Century show that Elstow Abbey held the patronage (the power to control appointments to office) of a rectory at Wilshamstead. Countess Judith had gifted this to the Abbey at the time of the Norman Conquest when she held the manor. By the 13th century, Elstow Abbey was one of the most prosperous Abbeys in the country and the Abbess and the Convent of Elstow became the first patrons of the vicarage. They nominated Richard de Leire (of Leicester) as first vicar in 1235. He was instituted to the new vicarage and was apportioned a fixed share of the

All Saints'
Wilshamstead

glebe land and tithes and received a perpetual endowment. All the ensuing vicars (as found in the list in appendix 1) received renumeration in the same way until the dissolution of the monasteries in 1539, during the reign of King Henry VIII.

The King confiscated large estates throughout the country, which he granted to friends and courtiers. All Saints' church under the patronage of Elstow Abbey passed to the Crown with a value of £25 13S 9¾d. Henry VIII retained all the manorial rights keeping the patronage vested in his own person. He leased his Wilshamstead property, which included the rectory, Church House and the glebe land to Edmund Harvey of Elstow in 1541. The King still reserved to himself the patronage of the church. Edmund Harvey's daughter married Sir Humphrey Radcliffe. In 1553 King Edward VI granted to Sir Humphrey Radcliffe, knight, 'all those our rectories and our churches of Elnestow, Wilshamstead and Kempston.' After this time, both the patronage and the advowson associated with All Saints' changed hands between many families.

Glebe land and tithes formed an important part of the church's history. The glebe land terrier of 1706 describes the glebe land as 'the lands that belong to the repair of the church and an account of the customes that belong to the vicarage of Wilshamstead.'

A tithe map of circa 1809 shows the church owning 2000 acres of all the land in the village. The Enclosure Act of 15th June 1809, for the parish of Wilshamstead states that Thomas Hind, clerk, his wife Ann and John Crosse Crooke are joint proprietors of three-fourths of all the rectorial or great tithes. They were awarded pieces of land equivalent on value to the glebe land they already held. The Act also states that Anthony Dauvert, vicar and his successors were entitled to the remaining undivided fourth part as a 'full equivalent and compensation for the glebe lands belonging to and enjoyed with the said vicarage.'

The basic structure of All Saints' church is made up of a chancel, a nave, north and south aisles, a vestry and a west tower. The walling is made of coursed ironstone and the ashlar work (masonry made of large square cut stones) is of oolite and chalk.

The Chancel is at the eastern end of a church. One of the most beautiful memorial windows in the church is the three light east window, depicting the Ascension. The stained glass panels were made by Clayton & Bell. A gift from Lord John Thynne, of Haynes Park Estate, it was placed in position when the chancel was rebuilt during restorations in 1872.

As early as 1404 restorations to the chancel took place, but our most detailed records date from the 19th century. In 1836 Archdeacon Bonney ordered that the walls of the church and chancel be cleaned.

Major restorations took place in the 1850s following a national movement to revive the bodies of churches. Mr Woodroffe of Bedford surveyed the church and made proposals to the Vestry committee to restore and repair the body of the church, erect a tower and increase the seating accommodation. The committee appointed to raise the funds included Rev F C G Passy (vicar), Abraham Burr, James Spring (churchwardens), Rev Lord John Thynne, John McDonald, Thomas

Interior of All Saints Church
with oil lamps

(Reproduced with the kind
permission of Bedfordshire and
Luton Archives and Records service)

James and Henry Peacock. Plans of Thomas Smith of 14 Hart Street, London were adopted on 23rd April 1851 and Walter Parker of Thrapston was accepted as contractor to carry out the work at a cost of £774. Finance was borrowed from the Exchequer Loan Fund and private subscriptions were also received. Lady Lucas had promised £300 and Lord John Thynne £100, and the parish raised £250 by rates. The work was completed and the church re-opened to its congregation on 2nd November 1851.

Later restorations to the church in 1872 were initiated by Reverend J H Macaulay. At the Vestry meeting of March 1872 promised contributions were announced from Rev Lord John Thynne, Mr W L Lowndes, Mr S Whitbread and Reverend J H Macaulay with a subscription list of all occupiers of land. A total of £1850 13s was raised. Sir Arthur Blomfield was appointed as architect and Mr J Osborn as the contractor. Some of the many restorations included an organ chamber, a new porch, cleaning of the roof of the nave, separation of the tower from the nave and a new pulpit.

The chancel was rebuilt and made 6ft longer than the previous one and the church also had new pews. On 24 April 1873, the Lord Bishop of Ely, Rev. Dr Edward Harold Brown re-consecrated the church.

Lord John Thynne gave an elaborate opus sectile reredos for the chancel. This opus panel was made up from ceramic pieces in a mosaic-fashion by Clayton & Bell in May 1873 with Powell of Whitefriars making the panels. The centre panel cost £47 5s and it depicted the Last Supper. The two side panels were of saints and martyrs and cost £25 6s 8d. This was placed in position when the high altar was added to the church. Unfortunately, at some point it fell off the wall and was replaced the following year in the same design at a cost of £75. Powell of Whitefriars later cleaned the reredos and because of 'the finish having gone bad' renewed the enamel free of charge in 1875. The reredos was removed in the 1960s. Unfortunately, it can no longer be found and is thought to have been destroyed.

In 1899 structural problems occurred in the chancel and the east end of the church was underpinned and the wall was rebuilt. In February 1900 part of the chancel had to be taken down and extensive work took place. This was surprising to many, because only 27 years had passed since the major restorations. Caused by subsidence and having been aggravated by consecutive dry summers large cracks appeared on the east and south walls and the roof had become badly displaced. The foundations were also found to be of poor quality and faulty. The chancel was out of use for a few weeks and church services were held in the nave. Use of the chancel for divine service began again on 11th March 1900.

Changes to the church took place in the 1930s when Reverend Harry Pollard agreed with Professor Richardson to restore the church to its medieval design. The changes included removing the coloured tiles in the chancel and replacing them with the present flagstones, although a few coloured tiles can still be found in the aisles.

The mound of earth to the west of the main church door contains the soil and debris from the chancel renovations. It cannot be removed because it is consecrated soil. Several choir stalls were removed along with the stone pulpit, which was replaced with the current wooden one.

On the south east of the nave wall, behind the Priest's stall is a 16th Century wall tablet of marble. It is to the memory of William Tompson of Wilshamstead born 25th February 1539 and buried in the church on 15th November 1596. William Tompson was the founder and a benefactor to the Wilstead Charities by a bequest made in 1596. In his will of 1596 it requested 'as concerning my body the same to be buried in the parish church of Wilshamstead in the middle of the alley there at my seat end.' In modern parlance the memorial reads:

> Here under lieth buried William Tompson who was
> Borne in Wilshamstead the 25th Day of February,
> Ano 1539, and was buried the 15th. Day of November,
> Ano 1596, the which William Tompson hath given in
> feofement by his last will and Testament five poun-
> Des yearly for ever to be paid out of a meadow
> Called Crosse Meade, a tenement wherein George
> Linford now dwelleth, the which five pounds is
> To be distributed to the poor of this parish of yea-
> Rely at the Feast of the nativity of Christ, fif
> Tie shillings, and at the feaste of the Resurrection
> Of Christe, other fiftie shillings, and to be dis-
> Tributed at the discretion of the minister, and
> Churchwardens for the time being for ever,
> Whose godly example God grant many to follow.
> He hath distributed and given to the poor his righteous-
> Nes remaineth for ever. Psalm. 112.9.
> Blessed is the man that considereth the poor and needy,
> The Lord shall deliver him in the time of need.
> **Psalm. 41.1**
> To doe good and to distribute, forget not for with such
> Sacrifices God is pleased.   **Hebrew. 13.16.**

The tablet also contains three inscriptions, unusually a mixture of Latin and English. The top and bottom are in Latin elegiac verses and the middle one is in English prose:

Top verse
> Viuo tibi, moriorq: tibi, tibi christe resurgam
> Morsq: mihi lucrum, tu mihi christe salus.

In English this becomes:
> To thee, I live, to Thee I die, to Thee,
> O Christ, again shall I arise,

Middle verse
> For e'en Thou, O Christ, to me
> Salvation art and death itself a prize.

Bottom verse
> Epitaphiv in obitum Gvlielmi Tompsoni,
> Mortua Tompsoni Gvlielmi membra tegvntur,
> Pvlvere svb simili conditione svmvs,
> Si qvid habent homines svperest virtvtis idipsum,
> Et bona stant dvo facta cadente svo,
> Qvuinque libros dedit hic qvas villae qvolibet ano
> Pavperibvs volvit tempus in omne dari,
> Caetera qvid memorem qvid oaetera mvlta recorder,
> Haec est agricolae fama relicta viri.

The parish magazine in 1904 recorded the translation of the bottom verse as:

> Epitaph on the death of William Tompson
> William Tompson's mortal parts lie in the dust entombed,
> And we though still above the ground to like estate are doomed.
> If men have aught of virtue's grace adorning fair their lives,
> When they have passed far hence away, 'tis that alone survives;
> Thus two almsdeeds in memory's ken shall fixed for ever stand
> By this man wrought, ere Death had clasped the donor's gen'rous hand:
> Five pounds, he willed, for benefit of Wilstead's worthy poor,
> Each year to be distributed thence forward evermore,
> Why should I tell of other boons?
> Why many more proclaim?
> Earth's tillers, behold above his legacy the man's fame!'

The £5 per annum mentioned in the inscription is part of his benefactions to the village, which totalled a bequest in excess of £100. This was added to the other small charities for the parish. His benefaction was referred to as the William Tompson Charity.

In 2000, with the help of several village organisations, the parish council, funds from the Millennium Fund and the Advent fayre, the damaged areas of the Tompson memorial were repaired and cleaned as part of the village Millennium project.

Several 18th century stone memorials are set in the floor in the centre aisle but are presently covered in carpet that is secured to them and are barely legible. In records, made by Reverend F C G Passy, he states that one of these 'in the centre of the middle aisle is a large stone to the memory of William Bedell, Esquire, who died in 1718. He was at the time the Lord of the Manor of Wilshamstead and Fenlake.'

The north arcade of the church belongs to the early 15th century and parts of the north aisle are believed to be 15th century rebuilt in the 19th century restorations.

Set into the wall between the vesting area (added in the 19th century restorations) and the north aisle is a piscina recess (basin in a niche) of the 15th century. This was for washing vessels used in the Eucharist service. An earlier piscina can be found on the wall of the south aisle. This has a trefoiled head and dates from the earlier 14th century.

On the north wall is a memorial to De Lacy Dayrell Passy, Captain 4th Regiment Madras Pioneers, born in the parish June 6th 1852 and died on February 3rd 1886 whilst serving his regiment at Dulojal in Afghanistan. The tablet was erected by his brother officers as a token of their esteem. He was the son of incumbent Frederic Charles George Passy whose surname was formerly Pawsey until it was changed by royal licence to Passy in 1842.

Importantly, for the village, All Saints' contains a rare ancient brass dating to around 1435. Sadly neglected and set into the floor beneath a pew at the east end of the north aisle, it represents a half-effigy of a priest, by the name of William Carbrok. The inscription is in very poor Latin. Containing rather obscure abbreviations, it reads:

Orate pro aia dni Willimi Carbrok Capellani ci'aie ppiciet' deus et pro aiab; Parentum patrum soror omniu benefactor' suor' et omniu fideliu defunctor'

William Carbrok brass 2002

In English this becomes:

Pray for the soul of Master William Carbrok the choirmaster, on whose soul may God look with mercy, and for the souls of his parents, ancestors, sisters, all his benefactors, and all the faithful departed.

The effigy shows a priest wearing an alb (white vestment reaching to his feet) with apparels (embroidered ornamentation) on the sleeves, a maniple (vestment strip) hanging from the left wrist and the top part of a chasuble (sleeveless outer vestment with a single hole for head). William Carbrok was not an incumbent but is most likely to have been a chantry priest. In this era special altars were added to a church where chantry priests might sing or chant mass daily for the souls of the founder of the altar and their relatives. Founders of these altars were county families who endowed religious houses because they wanted to be remembered in some way. Only the very rich people could fund chantries leaving others to give money for orbits (for the saying of mass annually for the repose of the soul) or money to have the name of the person placed in the beade roll and to be prayed for on certain occasions.

The origin of chantries dates back to the 13th century (contemporary with All Saints) but very few altars or chapels have been founded with the primary intention of perpetuating chantries. In Bedfordshire there were only three, one of which was Wilshamstead and in Tudor times, King Edward VI confiscated such endowments. Without endowment the chantry chapel would have fallen into disuse.

It is believed that the brass marks the resting-place of William Carbrok in the former site of the chantry chapel in the church. The significance and rarity of this ancient brass deserves to be restored and preserved for future generations.

On the north wall of the organ chamber is a brass plaque inscribed in remembrance of two former vicars. Reverend Frederic Passy, twenty years vicar of the parish, who died in 1843, and his successor and nephew Frederic Charles George Passy, died 1871, also vicar for 28 years. Both of these incumbents rest under unusual coffin shaped tombs in the churchyard.

A smaller brass plaque has been erected in memory of Arthur Wollaston Rose who died in 1887 during the South African war. He was vicar for three years.

Close to the north door is the font. As part of the Visitation Order of 1826 the Archdeacon Bonney ordered a new font basin which was eventually obtained 13 years later in 1839. By 1847 records show that 'the font of course has not escaped the usual disfigurement, the lead remains, but a trumpery basin is evidently used when the baptismal service is required'. Cleaning and fixing of the font with new steps formed part of the 1872 restorations. As one looks at the same font today, it appears that at some stage it may have had inscriptions around the centre but unfortunately these are no longer visible. It now also has a lid made of wood and lead.

Font 2002

The south arcade contains a coarsely carved stone head at each end. These appear to be leopard heads, believed to be the mark of royal reference, but no other history could be determined. The pillars on the south side, as you face the high altar, are far more irregular than those on the north side. It is believed that this is because this south side is the oldest part of the church and is 14th century in detail. Three plain windows in the south wall are 15th century in date. Special windows in the church remember members of the Coley, Cox, Gambriel and Craig families.

There is a war memorial window in the Lady Chapel on the south side to all the men of Wilshamstead who died in World War I. The window was completed in 1920 and designed by John Hall & Sons. To the left of the altar in the Lady Chapel is also a list of names of all that served in the armed forces. Deposited here are the standards of the Wilstead branch of the Royal British Legion.

A number of historic tablets are found in the church commemorating those who were originally buried within the walls. Many of these tablets have been moved from their original locations probably during the period of the restorations.

On the south wall of the south aisle is a simple marble tablet in memory of William Bull, a land owner who died on 23rd October 1820 aged 71 and who is believed to rest under one of the barely legible stones set in the floor.

In the west end of the church are several stone tablets in the walls of the tower to the memory of the Lucas family which inter-married with the Edwards family, one of the oldest parochial families who founded the Edwards Charity.

On the north wall of the organ enclave is a tablet in memory of William Edwards Esq. the only son of Ann and William Edwards Esq. He died 26 June 1758 aged 51, 'He left behind him one only child Mary by his beloved wife Dorothy who ordered this tomb to be erected out of pious gratitude to his memory'.

Set in stone in the floor beneath the south facing choir stalls in the chancel lies the body of William Edwards Esq. who died in 1731. The memorial tablet was originally on the wall in the chancel at the site of the tomb but the tablet was in later years moved to the west tower.

Mary Edwards married James Lucas and their remains are interred in a vault beneath the Church. The location of the vault is unknown.

In 1518 a parishioner left money for a new bell for the church and by 1707 Reverend Samuel Richardson recorded the church had four bells in the steeple plus a Saints bell, usually termed a priests bell or sanctus bell, a total peal of five bells. One of these 5 bells cracked and this was recast by bell founders Emmerton of Wootton in 1783. It is also understood that Emmerton recast the priest's bell in 1826. These 2 bells hang in the tower today. They are inscribed:

'EMMERTON OF WOOTTON FECIT 1783'
'GEORGE MORTON C WARDEN 1826'

Reverend Whitworth made a note of how the bell founder had misspelt the name of the churchwarden. The correct name was George Morgan but was inscribed as George Morton.

In 1990 Reverend Palmer discovered a bell in his garage inscribed with the date 1898. This bell had hung temporarily in the Infant school until finding a home at St Paul's Church, Littleworth, when its construction was complete. When St Paul's church was demolished the bell was taken to All Saints Church and at the time of writing it rests in the belfry waiting to be hung. The church may have also been given the school bell belonging to the church school when it was demolished in 1958, but its location is unknown.

Churches often have their own customs for the ringing of the bells. In addition to the church bells for Sunday services, in Wilshamstead the passing bell tolled solemnly after a funeral; thrice three tolls for a man, thrice twice tolls for a woman and thrice single tolls for infants. A bell was also rung after morning service and this was known as the potato bell. So called because on hearing the bell the people at home knew it was time to put their potatoes to the boil!

One may wonder, quite justifiably, why the church tower is so new compared to most other church towers when in many churches the tower is usually the most ancient part of the building. The current tower of All Saints dates to the church restorations of 1851 which is in contrast to the oldest part of the church dating from the 14th Century. The tale behind the 'newness' of the tower is tied up with the remaining three bells.

At 9.30 p.m. on Sunday 11th April 1742, the parish experienced a great gale sufficient to cause the church tower to collapse. Reverend John Gay obtained two estimates in July 1742. The first, to rebuild the tower and restore the damaged nave and aisles was £474 12s. The second to make good the damage in the church and to provide a temporary turret to hang up one bell, only amounted to £45. Wilshamstead was unable to raise the sum required for the full repairs and so on 17th September 1742, Richard Reynolds, the Bishop of the Diocese of Lincoln 'having considered the extent of the disaster and the inability of the parishioners to repair the steeple according to its ancient dimensions' gave permission for the less expensive repairs to be carried out. He granted a licence giving authorisation for the sale of three bells to meet the second estimate.

The churchwardens accounts for the sale of the bells and repairs of the church after the fall of the tower show a total income from the sale of the bells of £55 10 shillings. Local tradition says that the 3 bells were sold to Hendon Parish Church, in Middlesex.

Both enquiries made by Reverend Whitworth in November 1906 and exhaustive enquiries by the authors have found nothing to confirm the sale to Hendon. A recent investigation with the Diocese, Hendon Parish Church, historians and all parish records leads to the assumption that the bells were most probably sold for scrap metal. Thomas Russell, the Wootton bell founder, was particularly busy at that time and it is possible they were sold to him.

The church tower was rebuilt mainly of wood and was described as a 'cupola for a bell'. It lasted a little over one century. Whether it had deteriorated due to weather conditions or whether it had collapsed because it was only a temporary structure it is not certain. The present tower was built during the major church restorations of 1851. Walter Parker of Thrapston reconstructed it in ironstone according to his estimated cost of £670. The tower was separated from the nave, and the nave and aisles had to be reset.

On the tower are four bold gargoyles looking down from each corner. In medieval times the belief was that gargoyles would ward off any evil spirits but their main purpose was to act as a spout and drain water away from the wall of the building. The date of the Wilshamstead gargoyles is unknown but is likely to be a tradition carried over from the medieval beginnings of All Saints.

The clock was installed in the tower on November 25th 1898 at a cost of £96 to commemorate Queen Victoria's Diamond Jubilee. To celebrate this special day a public tea was provided in the schoolroom and a service followed by a choral evensong was held in the church under the clock tower. On the order of the service was:

> Dedication of the church clock; erected to the glory of God and to commemorate the Diamond Jubilee of Her Majesty Victoria, deigratia

and in the organ chamber a brass plaque shows the following inscription:

> The clock in this tower is erected to the Glory of God, and to commemorate 60 years of wise and beneficient reign, completed on June 21st 1897, by Her Majesty Victoria, by the Grace of God, Queen and Empress.
> The clock was dedicated and started Nov 25th 1898.
> Richard Charles Whitworth, MA vicar
> George Hallworth, Charles Hebbes, churchwardens.

The clock strikes on the hour on the larger of the two bells and was first overhauled on March 22nd and 23rd 1955. To this day its fine quality is maintained and serviced on a yearly basis. Currently every week, Mr John Pope dutifully climbs the narrow spiral steps to the belfry to ensure the clock is wound.

The timbered carved oak roof dates to the late medieval period and includes carved bosses and has carved figures of apostles all holding scrolls and resting on corbels. These figures of apostles would originally have had symbols showing below or in their hands but these are no longer there. Higher up in the roof one can see figures of angels and carved bosses.

Different parts of the roof have been replaced at various times and more recently it was restored in 1965, when extensive repairs to the nave roof took place in order to restore it to its former glory. Huge beams ravaged by dry rot had to be removed and replaced by English oak. Peter MacKinnon, a church joiner and wood carver from the village carried out the work. He specialised in church architectural woodwork and restoration of all types and his skill was very much in demand all over the country. He fitted the altar and pews and worked on the font in what is believed to be the oldest church in England in Escomb near Bishop Auckland.

In the south aisle of the roof at the west end one can see two wooden cherub trumpeters with a carved date of 1965 to mark the restoration.

The parish has in its possession a number of precious items of silver. The oldest a cover paten dated 1626 is exhibited at St Alban Cathedral's Treasury. The most recent piece is a silver chalice donated on May 1st 1994 by Reverend Roderick Palmer and dedicated by Bishop John, the Bishop of Bedford.

The surrounding churchyard provides its own record of history. Early entries recorded in the burial registers are:

1683   Mary Dow 'which was counted as a witch'.

1722	Jane Wilson, a travelling woman from Staffordshire was buried, May 14th.
1729	'a dumb stranger.'
1801	Burial. Smith Soloman 'an Egyptian or gypsy' March 8th.
1824	Burial. Thomas Kendall, Wilstead 26th March, 'died of the bite of a mad dog.'
1889	Burial. Frederick Redman, shot by misadventure, July 24th, aged 10 years.

Wilshamstead's Cup and Cover paten 1626

(Reproduced with the kind permission of St Albans Treasury)

Reverend Richard Charles Whitworth and his family have been buried here. Reverend Whitworth died on 23rd February 1947 and according to the churchwardens accounts, an extract from his will stated that £200 was to be kept in trust to keep the graveyard in good repair, especially regarding graves of himself, his wife and son Eric Charles Whitworth. Sadly today the cross memorial on the family grave is askew.

It was recorded that a 13th century coffin lid was found in the churchyard and which may have been of an early incumbent as one of similar character can be found in Elstow Abbey. The location of the Wilshamstead coffin lid is now unknown but lumps of loose masonry inside the church are purported to be part of it although this can not be verified.

In March 1900 the parish decided that as the graveyard was being filled steadily no further burials would be permitted in the churchyard except those who at their death were actual parishioners.

Following closure of part of the churchyard in 1976, kerbstones were removed and headstones straightened in order to simplify the maintenance of the area and arrangements were made to improve the path leading up to the site where the burials took place. The churchyard was full of 3-4 feet high grass and full of wild rose trees. The churchwardens levelled the ground with the help of local folk who had arrived with hooks and saws to help them with the laborious task. A churchwarden at the time recalled it was 'like painting the Fourth Bridge'. Their efforts were soon visible when the churchyard looked beautiful again. Shortly afterwards the maintenance responsibility was taken over by the Borough Council.

An approach to the Ecclesiastical Church Commissioners requested that some of their land be retained for future burials and finally a new area for burial was prepared for consecration and was dedicated in 1981. At a later date came the new larger modern burial ground adjacent to the churchyard.

In front of the church is the War Memorial, restored by the British Legion and public subscription in 1981, it stands in honour and remembrance of the men from Wilshamstead who had fought in both the World Wars and of whom many are buried on foreign shores.

The story of the church tower and its three bells is encapsulated in a number of versions of a rhyme. Both rhyme and tale inspired the current bowls club to use it as their emblem.

Wilshamstead folk are wicked people,
They sold the bells to build the steeple

There's a parish without any bells
For as ancient history tells
The good Wilstead people,
To build up their steeple,
Very wickedly sold the church bells

Wicked Wicked Wilstead people
Sold the bells to build their steeple.

Wilstead folks, wicked people
Sold their bells to build the steeple.

CHAPTER 4

The Name Game

The names we give to places often record aspects of history and heritage important to a village or town but as time and people move on the reason behind the name is often lost. For Wilshamstead, we have unearthed many of the meanings so that they can properly reflect the village history.

Where better place to start than with the name of the village itself.

WILSHAMSTEAD is the full and proper title of both the village and the ecclesiastical parish. A local colourful story is that the village was so named because William the Conqueror stayed here temporarily. Although his niece Judith held one of the manors, there is no evidence that William ever came here.

The parish is determined as an ancient parish because it was in existence before the Norman conquest in 1066 but the name was never recorded in writing until the Domesday book. Recorded in its true Anglo-Saxon spelling of Winessamstede, it is from this we understand the true meaning of Wilshamstead.

Winessamstede can be broken into its separate Anglo Saxon parts. Wine which means friend and pronounced Winny.

Millenium village gateway signs

Ham which means village and Stead which means place. Homestead of Friends. However it wasn't long after the Domesday book that the Norman practice of substituting an L for an N took place. Wine (Winny) was also an Anglo Saxon personal name and this has led to the corruption of the definition of – Wil's Homestead

This was the start of numerous spellings in the records over the centuries, often because written records were produced phonetically. People from outside the village wrote it down how they heard it and examples of the recorded names are:

Wilamstud	1181
Wyleshamstede	1220
Wilchamstede	1239
Wilshamstede	1240
Wilhamstede	1242
Wilsamstede	1247
Wilhampstede	1372
Willsamsted	1526
Wilsumstead	1675

The first shortened version of the name occurs in documentation in 1780 and it is likely that from this time the more easily pronounced Wilstead rose into popularity. The name of Wilshamstead fell into general disuse until the 1970's when the parish council resurrected the correct title but not everybody followed suit. The Ordnance Survey began a heated debate with the parish council which reached national notoriety when the issue was publicised in the News of the World Sunday newspaper in 1978.

Despite many of the road signs and maps still reflecting the strength of the popularised name, the village is now recognised formally under its true name of Wilshamstead.

Within the village itself, our road names reflect a variety of elements of the village history. It is important these are not forgotten and to record them for the future.

ARMSTRONG CLOSE

Part of the housing estate adjacent to Cotton End Road, this close was built in the 1960s. It was named after the Armstrong family who were prominent members of the village and whose achievements are recorded elsewhere in this book.

BEDFORD ROAD

This starts at the crossroads and runs north towards Bedford where it is divided by the modern A6 trunk road. Local reference is often made to the 'Bedford Road Loop'. This small section of Bedford Road which stretches from the A6 to Dane Lane, was isolated from the main body of the village by the bypass which replaced the main route through the village. The Bedford Road Loop may shortly form the outer edge of a proposed major housing development.

BLACK HAT CLOSE

This modern 1990s development was built on the site of one of Wilstead's oldest buildings, the Black Hat Public House whose frontage was of 15th century construction.

Black Hat Public House 1950s/1960s

This public house held the grand reputation of being the only pub in England with that name. It attracted plenty of myths, a female ghost who reputedly turned knives and forks upside down, Dick Turpin hiding in the cellar and associations with Puritans.

At the time a local name for a tiny adjacent side road was Milliners Close

BIRD COURT

The court acquired its name because a Mr Bird was involved with the development.

BRAMBLES

Named literally because the land was full of brambles.

BRIAR BANK MOBILE HOME PARK

The park was opened in 1957 and took its name from the adjacent Briar Bank Farmhouse (previously Darti Sharpe's Dairy Farm) upon whose land it was built. The park has a large selection of individual character homes set in avenues such as Honeysuckle, Laburnum and Oak Grove.

CASTLE CLOSE

This tiny road runs to the right hand side of the property that was once The Elephant & Castle Public House.

CHAPEL LANE

This small lane runs down to the site of the original Wesleyan Chapel built by the Armstrong family who were farmers at Manor Farm adjacent to Chapel Lane.

CHURCH ROAD

Leading up from the crossroads to the medieval church it is unlikely that the alignment of Church Road has changed over the years.

COTTON END ROAD

This road stretches across most of the parish. It is now so named because it leads towards the village of Cotton End. In the past various sections of it have held the names of High Street, Towne Street and The Street.

DANE LANE

In 1682 one of the village's open fields lay in the area close to where the current Dane Lane runs and this was called Dane Field. A trackway ran through to Dane Farm in Houghton Conquest and part of this became Dane Lane. A local story says the Dane name occurs in this part of the parish because it was the site of a Danish encampment during the invasions but to date there is no evidence to support this although there is a proven encampment at Bedford.

DINES CLOSE

This is located on land that used to be a tenement belonging to the Dines family who were farmers. The tenement, which would have resembled a small farm holding was the scene for the story involving James Addington reported elsewhere in this book. It was the involvement of this family, that brought the name of Dines to prominence in the village in 1832. Another family member, Joseph Dines, was a wheelwright in the village in the 19th century.

Land before Dines Close was constructed.
(Reproduced with the kind permission of Janet Brooks)

DUCK END LANE

Once a separate hamlet, the name of Duck End first appears in the village enclosure award. Duck End Pightle (which means small field or enclosure) is listed and was located in the earlier open field of Home Field.

There have been other village place names with animal connection in the village: Lamb Pits, Sheep Pit Close, Tench Brook, Hog Ditch and Lamb Pit Common but these have now fallen into disuse.

ELMS LANE

At the time of parish enclosure it was known as Thody's Lane. In the late 19th century, frequent reference is made to this road as Simms Lane as the farmer was Mr Simms at the bottom of the lane in Cotton End Manor Farm. At this time frontagers to roads in the parish had the right to allow their animals to graze on the herbage on the roadsides. The rent from this opportunity was collected by the parish and went to benefit the national school in Church Road. Simms Lane is recorded on several occasions as having an annual rent of 10 shillings.

In the early part of the 20th century this was referred to as Thorne's Lane as the farmer was Mr Thorne. The modern name derives from the lane being lined with Elm trees until they succumbed to an outbreak of Dutch Elm disease and had to be removed.

HAMPTON CLOSE

Part of the 1960s development adjacent to Cotton End Road, this close was named after Mr Frederick Hampton who was an early church school master and also the church organist. His wife also ran evening classes.

HOME CLOSE

Although of modern construction, it is possible it is so called because it runs towards the glebe land of the churchyard from which it would have been possible to gain access to 'Home Close'. The area of land where Little Church farmhouse is and the field beyond, where the Oakley Grange development is taking place was named in medieval times as Home Close.

HOOKED LANE

Pronounced locally as Hook-ed, this lane derives its name from its hooked shape. One of the oldest continuing names in the village, record is made in 1685 of Hooked Lane Furlong which would have run adjacent to it. This furlong would have been part of the nearby common open field of Home Field. In some parish minutes the lane is occasionally referred to as Crooked Lane.

HOWARD CLOSE

A modern development constructed in the 1990s it is named after Howard Sharpe who owned the land upon which it was built. The land formed part of his garden and a field he owned beyond. The Sharpe family have a long connection with this area of the village.

IVY LANE

It has been difficult to trace the history of this name. Although evidently taken from a proliferation of ivy at some location, the name was already established by the late 19th century.

LUTON ROAD

As with Bedford Road, Luton Road formed the main route through the village before the bypass and at one time the milepost for London was located at its beginning near the crossroads. Before the bypass, reference was also made to it as London Road.

MORGAN CLOSE

The achievements of our most famous village son, William Morgan, can be found elsewhere in this book but his name lives on within the development adjacent to Cotton End Road.

NORTHWOOD LANE

Originally this lane was occupied only by two farms, one farm at the very bottom of the lane and one on the east side. One being named after the Northwood family. Before this it was known as Pearce's lane.

PHIPPS CLOSE

This close is named after a prominent family of the mid 19th century. Mr Thomas Phipps ran a
grocery and drapery business
from a shop in the property to the
right of our current post office.
Mr George Phipps ran the Black
Hat Public House and also had
sufficient farming interests to
qualify him to be on the Jury list.
George Phipps junior, was a
butcher in the village.

Modern view of property where Thomas Phipps had his grocery shop (2001)

POLLARDS CLOSE

A long serving vicar of the parish was Reverend H P Pollard who lived in a property called Burystead House.

Burystead or Beristead house was located in the field opposite the small bridge (that still exists today) which ran from the churchyard. It is on this site that

Burystead House before demolition

(Reproduced with the kind permission of the Bedfordshire and Luton Archives and Records Service)

Pollards Close has been built. Known locally as Happy Harry Pollard he was of cheerful disposition and is remembered for his use of his phrase "Splendid, Rule Britannia, God save the Queen".

THE SQUARE

This original council house development takes its name from its style of construction and was built by Wilstead firm Gambriel and Sugars.

VICARAGE LANE

Similar to Church Road, this lane takes its name from its most prominent building. Now a modern vicarage is in place but previously a large imposing Victorian vicarage had its drive lead out onto the lane.

WHITWORTH WAY

Reverend and Mrs Whitworth were central figures in the village for many years. People still remember how he used to cycle with a carriage at the back of his bicycle.

Reverend and Mrs Whitworth and their son outside Victorian vicarage. The dog was called Jack.

(Reproduced with the kind permission of Brian Crouch)

WISSON COURT

The most recent construction in the village has taken place on the site of the 1960s tower block of flats. After demolition of the flats, sheltered housing bungalows have been constructed in 2002 and the court has been named after a prominent family of modern times who can be found throughout this book.

History also carries on in popular names and these are often never written down. The following examples are still in use in the village today.

CHAPEL END

Although not an end at all, this is the area of the village that clusters around the top of Chapel Lane and acquired its name by local reference.

DOGGETT'S LANE

If you are to stand at the very top of Vicarage Lane and look beyond the gate which stretches between the boundaries of the vicarage and Little Church Farmhouse you will be looking at a green ride that is still known as Doggett's Lane. This lane runs down to an area of land that used to form 3 fields in medieval times called

Ploughed Doggetts, Doggetts Close and Sward Doggetts. The Subsidy roll of 1332 records Willo Dogget as a Wilshamstead villager liable to pay tax and it is likely these were his holdings. The lane never had any legal right of way along it but many villagers recall walking along this lane to a connecting one, using it to get to ponds and playing on it as children. It was also a popular walk on a Sunday afternoon. In the 1980's following the closure of the donkey sanctuary at Little Church Farmhouse, new landowners constructed the gate which now stands and returned the usage only to those who have a right of way to the fields beyond.

HORTON TURN

In 1607 documents record Houghton Lane in connection with the open field called Hill Field. Hill Field lay to the rear of the current properties on the Bedford Road loop and was so called because of the slight rise in the land (The Knoll). Records assert it is likely that Houghton Lane is the road that appears on a number of 18th century maps but by time of enclosure it had disappeared. The line of Houghton Lane may be represented today by one of the ditches south of Horton Turn Farm because it is here that the boundary of Hill Field met the open field of West Field. Horton is the local phonetic representation of Houghton.

POTTER'S END

Many of the houses that cluster on Cotton End Road opposite the top of Elm's Lane used to be occupied by the Potter family and this area became known as Potter's End.

In 1891 Cotton End Farm was called Potters End Farm and was farmed by George Quenby.

STREET'S CORNER

A farming family of the name Street lived in the original Village Farm farmhouse further down the drive than the present buildings and thus the slight corner in Cotton End Road outside Village farm became known as Streets Corner. In the early 20th century, this corner became the dividing line between 'uptown' and 'downtown' and 'Church End' and 'Chapel End'. At this time, houses did not stretch the length of Cotton End Road as they do today. The division caused a few rivalries between the lads in the village. Although we cannot be certain, as no record was made, it is likely that the painting (see page 31) of a section of the The Street (early name for part of Cotton End Road) was created near to Street's Corner in 1820.

Other long forgotten names include Bug Row, Nether End, Tithe Lane and Great Lane.

Some of these names and plenty of others were set down in verse in 1890. The author is unknown but the recital was given by a Reverend G W Bowling at a Wilshamstead Parish concert. The proceeds of which amounted to £2 11 shillings and 6d.

Painting of The Street 1820

(Reproduced with the kind permission of Bedfordshire and Luton Archive and Records Service)

There's a parish without any bells,
For – so ancient history tells,
The good Wilstead people,
To build the church steeple,
Very wickedly, sold the church bells.

There's a Vicar of Wilstead called Whitworth,
Who is very much more than a bit worth,
In a chair he now sits,
And so sharp are his wits,
He deserves to be called Mr Whitworth.

Mr Whitworth has also a sister,
If she hadn't been here you'd have missed her,
For its plain that tonight,
You have heard with delight,
Miss Whitworth the good vicar's sister.

Mr Whitworth has also a baby,
As sweet a young cherub as may-be,
That infant is worth
All the treasure of earth,
He is such a magnificent baby.

There's a churchwarden Mr Geo. Hallworth,
A man who's by no means of small worth,
And the Wilshampstead Church,
Won't be left in the lurch,
While you've got Mr Churchwarden Hallworth.

His colleague you know Mr Cox,
He stands 5ft 8 in his socks,
In his socks or shoe leather,
In fair or foul weather,
To the front you will find Mr Cox

*A F C Cox butchers attached to The Nags Head
Public House*

(Reproduced with the kind permission of Dorothy Houghton)

There is also a Cox who's called Fred,
Who makes irreproachable bread,
His dough and his yeast,
Are as a good as a feast,
Indulged in by any crowned head.

There's a schoolmaster called Mr Hampton,
If you were to journey from Leicester to Campton,
You no-where will find,
A school master so kind,
Than that who we call Mr Hampton.

There's an Infants schoolmistress Miss Henshaw,
Her name as you know rhymes with Renshaw,
Who plays at lawn tennis,
But I'll bet six pennies,
He can't play a tune like Miss Henshaw.

You would find it the worst of disasters,
If Wilstead were robbed of its Masters,
For without a good clerk,
We are all in the dark,
And you've got a good clerk in Joe Masters.

There's a farmer who's name is George Redman,
A remarkably strong and well fed-man,
He towers over all,
And he is so very tall,
That wherever he goes he's a Headman.

There's a farmer who's come here from London,
Agriculture will never be undone,
While he remains here,
And its perfectly clear,
Mr Bottoms prefers this to London.

There's a farmer in Wilstead – James Newman,
He's true to his name and a trueman,
Joseph Newman and Ben,
We all know are true men,
And James is the right sort of Newman.

There's a jolly fellow called Boston,
I hope he will never be lost on-
Hill, Mountain or plain,
For we shan't find again,
A heartier fellow than Boston.

There's a Simms whom you all know,
His father is called Joe,
To look at he is good,
And its well understood,
That he's also a good one to go.

There's a capital wheelwright called Kendall,
He's a regular make all and mend all,
No wheels by the trade are so perfectly made,
As those manufactured by Kendall.

James Newman and Sons
hulling clover seed.

(Reproduced with the kind permission of
Brian Crouch)

Left to right: Ellen Kendall, Thomas Kendall, Mrs Elizabeth Kendall, Florence Kendall,
employee 'Jocka' Britten, with William Kendall at saw bench.

(Reproduced with the kind permission of Miriam Langford)

There's a king of blacksmiths, Jim Mastin,
He warrants his nails to stick fast in,
He succeeded to Tuffnail,
And you wont find a rough nail,
In the shoes made by Farrier Mastin.

*James Mastin and Emma Mastin with
three of their children.*

*(Reproduced with the kind permission
of Hilda Bourne)*

There's a grocer and draper called Phipps,
Up and down the country he whips,
And the village is blest,
Which so long possessed,
Two grocers like Tompkins and Phipps.

You've a shoemaker called Levi Potter,
If you wish to become a fast trotter,
Just put out you leg,
And be measured I beg,
For a pair of boots made by Potter.

Like his name Mr Sugars is sweet,
If you wish to go sound on your feet,
You never will meet a
Pair of boots that is neater,
Than those of that shoemaker sweet.

John Smith's a remarkable tailor,
No ploughman or soldier or sailor,
Will ever meet with,
Such a tailor as Smith,
The remarkable Wilshampstead tailor.

There's a road mender, old Thomas Daniel,
Who sticks to his work like a spaniel,
He fills up the holes,
And those diggers the moles,
Can't handle a spade like Tom Daniel.

I believe you all know Mrs Coley,
She gives up her time almost wholly,
To the Wilstead Post office,
At her work she's no novice,
Long life to our friend Mrs Coley.

Mrs Collins in Wilstead does well,
Rags and Bones and Hare skins she doth sell,
Now a donkey she owns
So her rags and her bones,
She finds it more easy to sell.

I had almost, if so I may say,
The toll-gate forgotten to pay,
You've a first rate machinist,
Mr Toll, who's the keenest,
Machinist, I'm told of the day.

My rhymes, you will find, dull I fear,
For I feel very stupid and queer,
But before you depart,
With the whole of my heart,
I wish you good luck through the whole of the year.

We parsons, we sometimes are told,
Are crusty and musty and old,
But we do what we can,
And the very best man,
Is made of the terrestrial mould.

So let us whatever the weather,
Pull a long and strong pull altogether,
Let us help one another,
Animosities smother,
Let mutual love be our tether.

One rhyme more. We've got a good queen,
Better monarch there never has been,
To the family royal,
We'er all of us loyal,
So we'll finish with GOD SAVE THE QUEEN.

CHAPTER 5

When I Was At School....

DAY SCHOOLS

Records of schooling in the parish can be traced back to the 16th century. An original assignment document from 1572 contains a schedule listing the uses and purposes of the property known as Church House in Church Road. With consent of the vicar and churchwardens it was to be used 'to teach and bring up young children in virtuous discipline, education and manners'. This meant it could be used as a parish schoolroom for the religious and elementary education of children.

This arrangement was formalised when the Endowed School opened in 1686 as a result of a benefaction of Reverend William Wells, vicar of the parish from 1662 to 1689. On November 3rd 1686 he bequeathed to the churchwardens and overseers of Wilshamstead £40 in trust to purchase land. This became the William Wells Charity. Ten freeholders of the parish were selected to act as a body of trustees to assist in the administration of this benefaction. The charity invested in 8 acres of arable land in the open fields and this in turn was to produce 40 shillings per annum for the purpose of educating the children of the village. The Endowed School was held in Church House. The charity provided the £8 11s 6d necessary to pay a school master to teach reading and catechism to as many children over the age of 4 who families could afford the small charge of 2d a week.

The will of 19th May 1703 of Dr James Johnson, a benefactor to many parishes, provided for an annual dividend to the parish The monies were used to purchase bibles, religious books and literature for the children and formed the beginnings of a more structured education system.

The Bishop of Lincoln visitation reports of 1717 and 1720 advised that although the Wells Charity was providing for the teaching of six children to read, there was no schoolmaster. The vicar was instructing them in catechism and taking them to church on prayer days but no other schooling was taking place. However, later in 1720, there was a new master and the endowment to him was shown as only £3 per annum. The attendance of scholars was an average between 18 and 20 per day.

The Edwards Charities were founded by benefactions of Richard Edwards in 1602 and by William Edwards in 1724. William left in his will a rent charge of £2 to be paid on the field called Town Close. This income from the field was to be paid half yearly to a schoolmaster for the benefit of schooling the children of Wilshamstead. The addition of the Edwards Charities to the Wells Charity allowed for a small schoolroom to be erected and schooling then moved away from Church House. This new schoolroom later became a small detached cottage, which in 1904 was occupied by Benjamin King and the site is now currently occupied by the garage attached to the Church House.

The schoolroom was the setting for a theft. The Quarter Session rolls of 1821-22 tell how Lucy Toll, a widow, who lived only 25 yards from the schoolroom, reported the break in. She said that at midnight someone had broken into the school, were inside for about 5 minutes and then ran away. Samuel Irons who lived nearby was awakened by a noise in the street of 'some person holloahing'. He got out of bed and went to his chamber window and heard somebody say 'be civil and harmless'. He then heard a noise as though a stone was being thrown against the school door. Together Lucy and Samuel went to report it to the schoolmaster who returned to the school with a light. The door had been kicked open and the marks of shoe nails were on it. Inside a staple was found on the floor and the desk had been broken open. At the hearing, David Whiteman testified that he had left the Red Lion and he was about 30 yards from the school when he saw James Redman smack his foot at the school door two or three times. Whiteman passed on and about 5 minutes later James Redman overtook him. Whiteman told the Quarter Sessions of how he had heard the door fly back even though he had not seen Redman enter the school.

The following day the schoolmaster missed about 100 pens and a cedar pencil which were later found in a field between Wilshamstead and Houghton Conquest. The schoolmaster advised the court that he used to keep money in the desk.

Education Returns of 1833 shows that of a population of 753, the Endowed School had an attendance of 34 scholars although only endowed with £8 0s 21/2 d per annum. This was only sufficient for the education of 16 scholars. The churchwardens and parish overseers nominated the 16 and the remaining attendees were at the expense of their parents.

The Wilshamstead National School was built in 1844 to cater for approximately 100 children. Lord John Carteret of Haynes Park Estate and his wife Mary Ann Carteret gave the school building, the master's house and the land upon which it was built. This was slightly further down Church Road from the earlier schoolroom. By 1851 there were a total of 58 children, 31 male and 27 female.

The school building was built of brick with a tiled roof. It consisted of a main room warmed by a tortoise stove, a classroom warmed by an open fire, a front lobby, a back lobby, separate girls and boys closets, coal barn and offices.

Girls Privy 2001

The adjacent schoolmaster's house was made up of a sitting room, kitchen, pantry and scullery with a staircase leading to 3 bedrooms. The water for both the house and the school had to be fetched from the village well at the crossroads with the use of a draw bucket. The school privies were either side of the schoolyard and the girl's privy still remains today.

On the 8th April 1852 the school was inspected and it was noted that: 'Organisation, four mixed classes, under master and monitors. Discipline very fair...Building excellent. Deficiency of books. Master intelligent and painstaking, and interested in his work. Religious instruction, good;...A pupil teacher would be great assistance to the master. There is no infant school, and the very young children who are received into this, require more immediate superintendence than is at present in the power of the master to give them.'

In 1870 enlargement of the school took place and further repairs were carried out in 1873 and 1877. By January 1883 Her Majesty's Inspection of Schools reported that the National School had 'improved both in numbers and attainments and the children now do their work satisfactorily.'

In 1888 a further room was added to the original building to provide further accommodation. In addition to the endowments the school received additional funds by means of voluntary contributions from the parish and monies from William Layton Lowndes, Esq owner of Church Farm.

In 1895 an order from the Board of Charity Commissioners directed monies from the School Charities to be spent annually in the form of money prizes and be presented to each scholar with regular attendance and good behaviour.

Prize Grading

GRADE I: For attendance equal to the number of times that the school was opened, each scholar received 4 shillings.

GRADE II: For attendance within 10 of the highest number possible, each scholar received 3 shillings.

GRADE III: For attendance not below 20 of the highest possible, each scholar received 2 shillings.

GRADE IV: For Attendance within 30 of the highest, each scholar received 1 shilling.

Due to the diminishing income from the charities, grade IV ceased in 1901.

The Inspector's Report for year ending November 1900 stated 'the general

Wilshamstead School Children circa 1905

(Reproduced with the kind ermission of Bedfordshire and Luton Archive and Records services)

efficiency of the school is very creditable. Reading, recitation, geography and drawing are well taught and the written exercises are exceedingly neat and accurate.'

Religion always played an important part in school life. In the early days from 1887 to the 1930s the Reverend Whitworth attended for weekly prayer, teaching religious education and questioning the children on scripture.

Sixty years after its construction the County surveyor reported on the condition of the school. The report had highlighted that due to the shrinkage of clay during the dry years there were serious fractures in the brickwork and it was in need of sound repair. The main room and classroom had poor ventilation and the floor in the main room was badly worn. The wall next to the lobby was badly fractured and the back lobby required more light and air. It was advised to extend the lobby into the yard with a sidelight and fanlight. It was necessary to renew all defective locks, fastenings and fittings. The offices were faulty and the girls' closets were dark and poorly ventilated, the boys' closets were damaged and both need to be replaced. The yard walling was in a poor state, its surface needed restoring and the roof had to be re-tiled.

The schoolmaster's house was also in need of decorative repairs as it was dark, damp and poorly ventilated. The front room required a wood floor with damp proofing. The stairway was very dark and in need of light. External repairs were also necessary to the roofs, walls and fences and all ironwork and woodwork needed restoring.

As a result the school was renovated. Around the same time the school was classified as a Public Elementary School but retained its denomination characteristic as a Church School.

Many local folk have spoken about their memories of the Church Road school. It was known to many as the top school. A typical school day would commence at 9 o'clock with the children all walking to the school. One notable exception to this was when Cotton End Road flooded and some of the children had to wait to be taken to school by horse and cart. The children's hands, nails and shoes were inspected on arrival and the teacher also checked that each child carried a hand-kerchief.

The main subjects were reading, writing and reciting poetry with a daily recita-tion of the timetables. Boys were taught gardening and girls attended sewing les-sons. Miss Hickling the headmistress, was regarded as a strict teacher and ordered the cane for children who had misbehaved. Very often the cane was given in pub-lic and in the presence of a Special Constable who would attend as a witness and adjudicator. After caning the child was sent home for the rest of the day. Miss Hickling was rather unique in her character and had a high pitched voice when telling the children to 'stop talking when I try to talk to you!'. Miss Hickling was a spinster and lived with her mother in the schoolhouse. Her mother always wore black clothes with a distinctive black pointed hat and these particular characteris-tics gained her the reputation of witch by the local children.

Physical education consisted of the children exercising in Church Road itself because the school play area was covered in cobbles. For gymnastics the girls just

School children at top school in 1950s

(Reproduced with the kind permission of Miriam Langford)

wore their tops and knickers. One lady recalls when the children were occa-sionally made to run from Luton Road to Vicarage Lane, past the church and back to the school in Church Road and referred to this as running 'round the triangle'.

Other times the children had to sim-ply hop three times and jump the once, however, the more mischievous boys can recall hopping three times and then jumping the once in a puddle, preferably when a teacher was standing close by. The purpose of this little scheme was in the hope that Miss Hickling would be absent from class for the rest of the day. Play times and physical education lessons were forbidden on days when a funeral was held in the village because of the school's proximity to the church.

During the Second World War the children attended school for half days only, in the mornings for one week followed by afternoons in the next week. This was because of the large number of evacuee children also attending school. At this time rooms in the Victorian vicarage were also used for teaching.

The school closed in 1958 and was demolished in 1973. One local can recall the day of the demolition as the same day as Princess Anne's wedding.

The site was partially used for the development of 2 houses, one which today is called the Old Brick House. The school was replaced by the existing Local Education Authority Lower School in Cotton End Road.

Many children had to walk long distances to get to and from the school in Church Road. To spare the little ones journey by foot, an Infant School was

*National School
(Top School)*

*(Reproduced with the kind permis-
sion of Bedfordshire and Luton
Archive and Records Service)*

opened in 1873 on Cotton End Road opposite Northwood Lane.

The Reverend Lord John Thynne, the successor of Lord John Carteret, paid for the school and it remained in his ownership, leasing it for an annual rent.

The bricks used in the construction of the school were made at the Wilshamstead brickwork's at Dane Lane. The school consisted of two rooms open to the rafters with small windows and little light. It was heated by an open grate and a tortoise stove. There was another fireplace in the lean-to cloakroom.

The school bell was in an elaborate timber framed lobby porch. The yard had a barn and a coal store. The wooden privy was common to both boys and girls and was located at the bottom of the garden path.

The water supply came from the well at the nearby school mistresses cottage.

To the left of the school, still standing today, are a pair of 18th Century cottages that are partly timber framed with pebbledash render and partly mottled brick. These are believed to have been built for the purpose of providing a home for the school headmistresses. When the infant school was inspected in the year ending 30 November 1900 it was reported that 'The school is taught with much care and intelligence, and with very creditable success and the excellent discipline and training and happy tone of the children deserve the highest praise.'

*School mistress house
and infant school*

*(Reproduced with the kind permission
of Janet Brooks)*

Interior of infant school circa 1937–1939

(Reproduced with the kind permission of Ken Green)

The discipline was carried on when Miss Fanny Plumb aged 25 was appointed as headmistress on 23 June 1904. From a collection of letters and references exchanged between her and Reverend Whitworth, we know that she was a 'good disciplinarian and very energetic and successful worker.' She stayed in temporary lodgings at Church Farm before moving to the schoolhouse. Her salary was £75 per annum and she made arrangements to have a maid attend to her.

The Infant school children could receive prizes in the same way as the National school in Church Road for regular attendance and good behaviour and like the larger school it retained its denominational characteristic as a church school when classified as a Public Elementary School in 1903.

Memories of the school in the 1920s recall how the children were taught how to draw pot hooks (shape of a letter S) on slates with a slate pencil and the times when they drew with their little bare fingers in trays filled with fine golden sand. Children would also be given mock shoelaces and they had to learn how to lace up shoes. The earliest recollection of hymns sang at the school was that of 'There is a green hill far away' and 'Lord keep us safe this night, secure from all our fears, may angels guard us while we sleep until morning light appears' which was sang at the close of day.

May Day was a popular event at the Infant school. In the early 1900s May Day was held on the vicarage green.

May Day on vicarage green circa 1910

(Reproduced with the kind permission of Miriam Langford)

It was an honour for the girls to be chosen as May Queen for their school. Since the 1920s it had been customary for the children to submit a written vote for the May Queen of their choice, even though one suspected that the teachers had the final say.

From the mid 1930s May Day was held at the top of Northwood Lane and later in Mrs Crawley's garden, on the corner of Chapel Lane which is a small copse today. The original chapel can be seen through the trees on the photograph.

May Day of 1945 was particularly remembered as a special event to commemorate the end of the war. The little children walked behind the horse and cart to Mrs Crawley's garden carrying their crepe-coloured flowers to the maypole where they would perform the traditional dances.

In later years the May Queen would sit on the headmistresses chair on Mr 'Darti' Sharpe's float surrounded by two or three attendants. Mr Sharpe then proudly drove the chosen May Queen back to the school.

At the time of the Second World War the children had to carry gas masks to school and in the event of an air raid the children obeyed the strict instructions and ran to the air raid shelter near the school.

Infant School headmistress Miss Lilian Whyley is long recalled. Described as very prim and proper with a reserved personality, she never raised her voice, she was fairly strict and did not tolerate any form of misbehaviour leaving the children convinced she had eyes in the back of her head when she stood at the blackboard. Although she never used the cane, Miss Whyley made children wash their mouth out with carbolic soap if they swore and one gentleman can still describe the experience today.

May Day in Northwood Lane circa 1930
(Reproduced with the kind permission of Ken Green)

May day in Mrs Crawley's garden late 1940s
(Reproduced with the kind permission of Joan Elkins)

May Fay 1945
(Reproduced with the kind permission of Joan Elkins)

May day at Infant School 1946,
June Cooper May Queen

(Reproduced with the kind permission of Janet
Brooks)

In 1946 the school was classified and named as the County Primary Infant School. It closed in 1958 when the new County Primary School opened. The Infant School building was converted into a private residential dwelling in the 1960s and it has been renovated again recently.

Following the closure, the school hand bell was gifted to Arthur Mastin Sharpe (Darti Sharpe), who was the owner of Briar Bank Dairy Farm. He was a long serving member of the Parish Council and had been a Special Constable of the village. The bell remains in the family.

The buildings of Wilshamstead Primary School under the control of the Local Education Authority were opened on 24th February 1958. When pupils from the Church Road School and the Infant School finally merged on 21st April 1958 there was a total number of 64 children on the school roll. Miss E M Rimes was the school headmistress having previously taught the juniors in Church Road. She can be found in the list of school teachers at Appendix 2. The school building consisted of three well furnished and equipped classrooms, staff rooms, kitchen and ancillaries. The three classes were made up of 27 infant children with Miss Rimes, 21 lower juniors with Miss Stevens and 16 upper juniors with Miss Emery. The first school holiday took place just a month later on the May 21st 1958 when it shut for half a day to celebrate Empire Day.

The first school inspection was on December 2nd 1958 when it was reported that 'there is significant improvement in the attitude of the children and in their progress, socially, intellectually and musically.' This was in comparison to the previous two schools in the village. The school's first birthday was celebrated on 21st April 1959 and a telegram of greeting was sent to Her Majesty Queen Elizabeth II.

An outdoor swimming pool arrived on 17th March 1965. The children had raised £88 towards the cost of the pool by selling scent cards and arranging jumble sales and whist drives. A youth club concert held over 2 nights also raised £33. Major E J Howard OBE officially opened the pool on 22 July 1965 and the children gave a swimming display to a large audience.

At the time, Julia Morgan aged 11 wrote about the school swimming pool, 'Everybody changes as fast as they can and then they run out of the toilets and jump into the swimming pool. Sometimes it is cold and you cannot get in but when you swim about it is lovely. On some days a Mrs Watson comes and then we can stay in until about half past four. When we get out we go and change and we are

May Day 2001

lovely and warm.' The swimming pool was removed in the 1990s.

In April 1971 the school had 183 children on its roll and on 1st September the school was re-named as Wilstead Lower School. The lowering of the age for transition to middle school changed in 1971 and this eased the overcrowding. A school extension was also built later that year.

The end of the 1973 academic year was celebrated with a historic exhibition and pageant of Wilstead. Mr Patrick Shallard, the Chief Education Officer opened the pageant and exhibition on 3rd July and 50 children performed a pageant to an audience of over 400 people. The exhibition was mounted in the three classrooms of the original building and displayed many historic items from the village including farming implements, clothes, lace and photos.

The first school May Day celebration recorded for many years took place on 21st May 1975 under the leadership of the new headmaster, Mr Anthony Riley. The whole school paraded through the village and then gave displays of singing and maypole dancing.

The school has maintained the tradition of May Day and parents are annually invited to watch maypole dancing.

In September 1986 the current headmaster, Mr Stephen Elphick arrived at the school which had a total of 90 children in five classes. The school is currently divided into two main teaching areas, the hall and the administration block. There are two playgrounds and a large grassed area around the school enabling the children to play with others of their own age group.

EVENING SCHOOLS

In the Victorian period, evening schools were held at the Church Road School by Mr and Mrs Hampton and became known as the Evening Continuation Classes. These were overseen by the Board of Education. The boys attended on Monday and Wednesday evenings and the classes were conducted by Mr Hampton. The girls attended on Tuesday and Friday evenings and classes were conducted by Mrs Hampton.

At the end of the winter session, social evenings were arranged for the scholars and teachers. Scholars received rewards for regularity and good conduct and in June 1900 the Board of Education advised that the females had earned the superior grant and the boys the lower grant.

In July 1901 the following report was written about the night schools:

> Boys School: 'The discipline is good and sound practical work has been done in arithmetic. Composition should improve.'
> Girls School: 'The discipline and instruction are praiseworthy and very creditable and progress has been made during the past session.'

SUNDAY SCHOOLS

The Education Returns of 1833 showed two Sunday Schools existed. At one point the All Saints' Sunday School had 60 children of both sexes attending.

The other Sunday school, with an attendance of 50 children of both sexes, belonged to the Methodist Chapel. The Wilstead Methodist Church preserves their Minute Book of their Wilshamstead Sunday school established in January 1826. The Sunday school had a number of rules to adhere to. One of these was 'That every scholar for attending on time shall have a ticket. When they have 12 tickets they may have a token or small reward book and when they have 6 of these said tokens they shall have a Testament. Only when they have four and twenty tokens they shall have a Bible.'

The importance placed on catechism schooling by the Methodists was shown in October 1826 when it was agreed that every absent teacher should forfeit 6d and any absent Superintendent should forfeit 1 shilling. There were a number of other forfeits that could also be given. No teacher was 'to be suffered to continue in this school unless they regularly pay up their forfeit money.' Female teachers were to attend once in 3 weeks and male teachers once in a month. Many of the teachers seem to have come from long established Wilshamstead families. A list of some of the Methodist Sunday school teachers can be found at appendix 3. By 1834 it was agreed that the rules of the school were to be made public. Prayer meetings were held monthly and females would meet separately from the males.

The income collected from the forfeit system was used to purchase pencils, slates, paper, spelling books, tokens and tickets in addition to bibles and testaments.

LACEMAKING SCHOOLS

To supplement the family income young girls in the 19th Century attended lace making schools where a little reading would also be taught and occasionally other lessons.

The children purchased their own materials and the teacher sold the lace and paid the children for the work they had done. Girls of 9 to 10 years of age could earn 1 shilling a week.

The H M Inspector of Schools reported on two lace making schools in Wilshamstead in 1849. Mrs Cox held the first. The classroom measured 14 × 12 × 6.5

Wilshamstead lace makers

(Reproduced with the kind permission of Brian Crouch)

feet with one fireplace and three windows, which could not be opened.

The room allowed for 20 girls aged between 7 and 14 plus the mistress. The girls worked from 7am to 5pm in the summer and from 8am to 8pm in the winter with one hour to return home for dinner. The elder girls would stay and work by candlelight until 9pm and others would take their pillows and horses (pillow stands) home to work on at night.

The inspector's report on one girl who attended was Mary Pearce, age 10: 'Here two years.... learned sewing and reading at school before, but did not learn writing, summing, or figures. (Spells one syllable words.). Does not know what "gay" or "king" means and has not heard the queen's name. Does not work at home. Has taken 1s 8d home to mother in a week for three collars.'

The teachers were strict and insisted that the lace was kept clean or the cane would be administered. A bag of starch was kept close to the girl's working area so that they could dip their fingers into the starch so that they would keep clean.

The second school was held by Mrs Smith whose usual number of attendants was 23 in a small room measuring 10.5 × 10 × 6.5 feet. Most of the girls had started at the age of 6 and they would not earn anything in the first 6 months. The little ones worked for 6 hours a day and girls over the age of 11 worked for 12 hours. A girl of 13 years was capable of earning 2s 3d in a week when the price was low but could earn double this amount if the price was high.

Two comments by the Inspector on Mrs Smith's school reported:

'Jane Alcock, age 9. Here a year, leaves at 4.40 in the afternoon. Was at school for half a year only, and never has been on Sunday. Learned reading, writing and sewing but no figures. Spells "do".'

'Elizabeth Bar, age 8. Lately come here, but was at her aunt's lace school before. Was never at any other kind of school, except the Sunday to which she still goes. Cannot read.'

The Workshop Act of 1867 eventually closed the lace schools because no child under 8 could be employed and from the age of 8 to 13 they were only allowed to work part of the day. The legislation for compulsory education in 1871 ensured that children employed in workshops also had access to school education.

Whilst the girls were working they would sing lace tells. Although no rhyme specific to Wilshamstead has been found, an example of a lace tell is below. These songs were used to help the girls with their counting in the lace making process.

Twenty pins have I to do
Let ways be ever so dirty
Never a penny in my purse
But farthings five and thirty

CHAPTER 6

Wilshamstead – The Second Millennium

We begin our second trip through the ages at the time of the Norman Conquest. Following the defeat of King Harrold at the Battle of Hastings in 1066, William the Conquerors army swept across the country and Anglo-Norman rule began.

Sweeping up the Icknield Way to the south of Bedfordshire, the army went on to seize manors and property before taking the town of Bedford. To feed itself on route, supplies of meat and corn for the men and food for the horses were levied from the villages it passed through. The provision of these supplies would have included the necessary corn and oxen needed for the following year's crop. When valued a year later, villages on the route of the march had been reduced to less than half their previous value. Any resistance to the provision of the supplies met with the reprisal of an increased levy.

Wilshamstead villagers must have felt very strongly about giving away their provisions and resisted because when the parish was assessed it was worth 21% of its original value.

The most famous valuation took place under William the Conqueror in 1086. The Domesday Book was the result of a survey commissioned by the king to determine who lived in the villages and what they owned.

Winessamstede was recorded as having a population of 23 men for valuation purposes with the land in the ownership of two Lords of the Manor, Countess Judith in the east and Nigel D'Albini in the west of the parish. In addition Ordwy, the Kings reeve (local official) owned a virgate (normally around 30 acres) in the west of the parish with a value of 5 shillings. This supported 1 smallholder, 1 slave and 5 oxen and had been in his possession at the time of the conquest in 1066 and was still in his holding in 1087.

Manors were the basic unit of feudal landownership. As manorial jurisdictions did not necessarily match parish boundaries, a parish could have more than one manor and thus more than one Lord of the Manor.

The first written record of the two Wilshamstead manors in the Domesday Book shows us how the land came into the transferable ownership of the lords of the manor. All land belonged to the Crown unless it was granted in exchange for services. William the Conqueror granted lands to his niece, Countess Judith de Balliol, which included Wilshamsteads principle manor of the main village. The smaller manor of Westcotts, located between the main village and Eastcotts was acquired from socmen (free peasants) for Nigel D'Albini. Along with lands in near-by parishes this grant was to enable him to fulfil his baronial obligations of providing 25 knights for the service of William the Conqueror.

The early lords maintained local customs and regulations, managed the land and its use and controlled the behaviour of the tenants but the Lords of the Manors were not themselves beyond the bounds of justice. In 1652, Lord of the principle manor, John Manley, appeared in court and was fined 3 shillings for 'speaking scandalous words of Robert Lovell Esq., JP'.

The history of the two manors follows like a traditional history lesson with names and dates and places so the succession of the ownership over the centuries has been related in Appendix 4.

Little else is known about Wilshamstead under Norman rule and so we move onto the Middle Ages.

Few details exist about the individual inhabitants of the parish in this period but records of one serious crime tell us about Simon, a Wilshamstead villager.

Roger le Bole was convicted of 'divers felonies' (diverse crimes) by the Bedford Gaol delivery justices and on 12 November 1303 he was hanged by Henry Bobbe of Lower Caldecote at gallows near Biddenham.

As Henry returned to Bedford he was attacked. Thomas, son of Gervase the cobbler, gave Henry three blows with his hand and Simon, son of Roger le Bercher of Wilshamstead, struck him between the shoulder blades with a blackthorn staff. Unable to go any further, Henry sat down in William Bascat's croft (an enclosed field) but Richard of Old Warden struck him in the chest with an iron fork and Henry died immediately. This field was under the wall of the Friars Minors of Bedford. These were the grey friars monks that settled in Bedford in the 13th century and who are still represented in the Greyfriars street name and area of Bedford today.

The three attackers fled but it was apparent that there was a larger group of men nearby. When Ralph le Webbe found the body and raised the hue, he was attacked by Peter de Merton and John le Bole. Neighbours responding to the alarm were also assaulted. Simon Ravenyg was attacked by Roger Sourdow and Robert le Corder; Walter the clerk by Robert le Webbe and Richard Dye; Walter Scotard by Ralph le Toller and Guy le Tournour and Robert le Corder by Geoffrey le Lavender and Nicholas Messer.

Simon, son of Roger le Bercher of Wilshamstead, was arrested for the death of Henry Bobbe and imprisoned in Bedford gaol. He broke out however and fled to St Paul's Church. Stating before Nicholas Feron, coroner of Bedford, that he was at the death, he swore an oath to leave the country forever and thus avoided trial.

An Eyre was held. This medieval court, where a judge travelled from county to county for the purpose, ordered that Thomas, son of Gervase the cobbler and Richard of Old Warden be obtained and outlawed as they were strangers with neither property or tithing (not belonging to a Hundred). As Simon had escaped, judgement was passed against the tenants of the lands of the Sheriff. Additionally, by the time of the Eyre both the finder of the body, Ralph le Webbe, and his neighbours had also died and murdrum was imposed on Bedford. This was a collective fine for failure to apprehend the criminals.

Surnames of the 14th century reflected either a person's abode, status, occupation or his father or ancestor. The murder case clearly shows many occupations but the subsidy rolls for Wilshamstead show surnames reflecting abodes.

The Wilshamstead Subsidy Roll for 1309 shows 34 freeholders of land eligible to pay tax. King Edward I needed to raise money for his campaigns and requested a subsidy. A medieval subsidy was a parliamentary grant made to the sovereign for state needs. The money was raised through taxation and a subsidy roll shows the people who qualified to pay the tax and the amounts.

In 1332 King Edward III wanted to carry out reforms and the tax list of villagers shows the number of freeholders had diminished to 29.

Reverend Whitworth converted the 1332 subsidy into the terminology of the 19th century and it is notable that one parishioner had the surname Passy. In the 19th century the Passy family held the position of vicar for two succeeding generations.

Both subsidy rolls are recorded in Appendix 5.

By 1340 more money was needed, this time for the wars against France and Scotland. King Edward III passed an Act of Parliament that would allow an enquiry of parishioners through appointed commissioners to find the value of the ninth lamb, fleece and sheep to find who could be taxed. This was the 'Nonarum Inquisitiones' or Enquiries on Nones. Wilshamstead's appointed commissioners were William Doget, Simon Calnehulle, Roger Lamb, William Asseylyne, John Heyroun and Gregory Saltiel. They reported that a Prior of St Beaulieu (likely to be St Macute's Chapel) was assessed at 10 marks and that the church held lands and tithes that were taxable. They attested however, that there were no other citizens, merchants or other people farming that had goods or chattels upon which tax could be levied.

> **DID YOU KNOW?**
> Sheep farming continued in the parish. A medieval bronze crottel or crotal bell was discovered in the fields of Village Farm by the Crouch family. In the thirteenth century, these fields were a wide open space, grazed by large flocks and the bells were used as a means of identification.

Along with many other villages the plague visited Wilshamstead and it is thought the village was particularly badly affected by the Black Death in 1349–1350. A local story says the part of the village that was affected, was clustered around the fields of Doggetts Close, Ploughed Doggetts and Sward Doggetts at the bottom of Doggetts Lane.

The authors have taken expert advice on this subject which deems it unlikely that occupation was in this area. The fields were intensively farmed and even today the ridge and furrow of the medieval techniques are still clearly visible. With so much medieval arable activity the homes of the villagers were most likely further away, probably around the nucleus of the village green. The story may have its roots in the fact that earthworks, containing two rectangular enclosures and a mound, exist in Doggetts Close. This is possibly evidence of occupation activity at one time but not necessarily at the time of the Black Death.

In the Tudor period, a number of 'Wylsampsted' men were mustered in 1539. These men were bylmen with a weapon derived from the agricultural tool, the bill-hook. It was the principle weapon of the English infantry in the sixteenth century, despite developments in armour and firearms in Europe.

At the end of that century Thomas Cooper of Wilshamstead was impressed into service in December 1598 for service as a pikeman in Ireland as Queen Elizabeth I fought for control of Ireland.

By virtue of a writ of 19 September 1637, Bedfordshire was levied to provide £3000 for the provision of a ship of 300 tonnes. This tax was split between the parishes. But only a single Ship Money list still remains.

'Wilshamsteede Shipmoney 1637' lists the people who suffered the levy to raise £25 10shillings 11d. Many family names crop up regularly in the history of the parish and some of these feature in the list. Surnames such as Cawne (Cawne Close) and Doggett (Doggetts Lane). The list has been produced at appendix 6.

Although various taxes were levied upon property holders, a number of benefactors in the 16th–18th centuries were able to make long term provision for the people of the village, in the form of charity. These charities albeit in a different form, are still ongoing and are currently governed by Wilshamstead Endowed Charities. The benefactions provided money for the church, the poor and schooling.

WYLSAMPSTED BYLMEN 1539
John Adam
Robert Arde
John Astlyn
John Dawker
Richard Edward
Henry Francklyn
John Hebs junior
John Hebs senior
Thomas Hebs
William Kawme
Thomas Negusse
Thomas Nores
Richard Page
John Palmer
Henry Palmer
Thomas Parker
Richard Pawmer
Philip Purser
John Smythe
Thomas Tailour
William Woode

WILSHAMSTEAD ENDOWED CHARITIES

Main benefactions included:

Early 16th century, benefactor unknown – Crowsley's Field for Church Charity
Henry Sims, benefactor – church charity

1596	William Thompson – Crossmead field for poor charity
1686	Reverend William Wells - Schools charity
1693	Thomas Hillersden – poor charity
1703	Dr James Johnson – book gift for school charity
1716	Mary Beech – poor charity
1724	William Edwards – schools charity

The English Civil War broke out in August 1642 when King Charles declared war against parliament and a few effects of the civil war on the parish were recorded.

A warrant of July 1644 required that 100 horses be commandeered from the 14 parishes of Redbornstoke Hundred. The horses were to be provided with saddles and bridles for the service of Sir William Waller and 7 of these horses came from Wilshamstead.

INVENTORY OF RICHARD SHARP	2 May 1775
1 longhook	1 shorthook
1 hatchet	1 rake
2 forks	bellows
4 chairs	1 table
1 strawbed	1 bedstead
1 flockbed	1 iron pot
1 blanket	2 shirts

In 1648, an ordinance issued by the Parliamentarians confiscated the estates of two groups, royal recusants (those people who were both loyal to the crown and who refused to attend church of England services) and catholic delinquents (papists). English Catholics had been persecuted since 1570 and all Catholics were still considered to be potential traitors.

Elizabeth, Margaret and Anne Mordaunt held both of the Wilshamstead manors and these lands had produced a total rent of £199 in 1647. As papists, however, their lands were sequestered under the ordinance and 2 parts were given to a Mr Pitkin. Being of poor health he wanted to give them up, so Captain Smith was appointed by committee to let the land to Robert Little of Bedford. He was requested to negotiate the best value he could agree for the best advantage of the state.

The next era of change took place in the 18th century when increasing industrialisation placed the poorer members of society under greater pressure. The Poor Law Commissioners gave four types of relief to those in need: money, clothing, food or miscellaneous requirements. An example from the 1771 Wilshamstead accounts include 1 shilling 6 pence for an apron for Mr W Bird; 2 pence for a pint of beer for Mr M Ball and 2 shillings 6 pence for a midwife for Sarah Fisher. To ensure the applicant was genuinely in need an inventory of their belongings was sometimes made.

Wilshamstead men continued to muster to the militias as the centuries passed. 1683 saw 9 Wilstonians in The Collonells Company, 5 bearing muskets and 4 wearing corslets. By 1783, the militia was partly formed by

DID YOU KNOW?

A 17th century corslet was light half armour designed to protect the torso. It consisted of a gorget (collar); breastplate; backplate; gauntlets; tassets (pliable iron or steel plates of sliding rivets to protect the upper thighs) and an open helmet.

(Reproduced with the kind permission of the Royal Armouries)

enrolment and partly by lot with families such as Kendall and Green listed. By 1831 William Litchfield is shown in Captain Higgins Company as being from Wilshamstead aged 23 with no children.

Parish boundaries were traditionally maintained by beating the bounds. In 1703, for Wilshamstead this involved processioning on 9th May, starting at Budmore Hole thence to Hardwick and right round to the start. 31 boundary markers were renewed at a cost of 17 shillings 6 pence. Beating the bounds continued periodically until the late 19th century when parliament made a number of acts to permanently determine the boundaries. Wilshamstead's enclosure act was made in 1809 with the awards being made in 1811. After this time many of the names and reference points changed.

After the enclosure commissioners had granted parcels of land to the Lords of the manor and the vicar, the remainder was assigned to the ordinary people. The proportions were determined in respect of the amount of their loss of strips in the open fields, their rights of common and their inability to keep stock anymore. Despite 108 dwellings in the village, only one cottager, Thomas Liles, had a successful claim for common rights showing that much of the land was already in a few ownerships.

The previously open fields to the north of the parish were enclosed with 'quickset hedges and ditches, or other proper mounds or fences, with proper post, rails and other guard fences'. Within the enclosed fields, 2 gravel pits were retained for the use of the parish but by 1850 supply of gravel was being obtained from elsewhere and by 1862 the pits were sold to Lord John Thynne and Reverend Venn. At some point ownership of the pits was returned to the parish. Unfortunately, failure by commoners to exercise their rights for a period of at least 30-40 years meant they lost their right to access and gravel extraction. A decision was taken by the parish council in 1968 not to register them as common land.

BEDFORDSHIRE TOLL CHARGES	
1 horse, mule or ass laden or unladen (not pulling)	1 1/2 half pence
20 calves, hogs, sheep or lambs	6 pence
20 oxen or neat cattle	20 pence
1 –3 horses	1 shilling
Coach, chariot or chaise drawn by 1,2 or 3 horses	1 shilling
Coach, chariot or chaise drawn by 4 – 6 horses or more	1 shilling 6 pence
Waggon, cart or carriage drawn by 4, 5 or 6 horses	1 shilling 6 pence

The Bedford to Luton road had been turnpiked at Haynes turning, just beyond Wilstead Hill in 1767. Following the enclosure of the parish, the village roads were improved so much that Samuel Whitbread remarked 'There is now very little road in [that] parish but what is in a complete state'. The improved roads meant that heavy traffic sometimes took to the side roads to evade the toll at the turnpike. In 1814, John Morris, an Ampthill brewer, promised to make amendment when his wagons detoured regularly through Wilshamstead and had a serious effect on the surface.

As unemployment increased and conditions for labourers worsened, early Victorian villagers were encouraged to emigrate. The money had to be raised for the passage, sometimes privately, sometimes from the parish. £40 10 shillings was required in 1845 for the emigration to Canada of Benjamin Litchfield, his wife and child; Daniel Simms, his wife and child; Richard Simms and William Watts. The money was provided from the Poor Rate. Writing to Reverend Passy, they said they had arrived in good health and the ship was clean and in good order.

In 1853, Mr George Rogers emigrated to the United States and the following year sent £20 towards the cost of the passage for his wife and four children. The parish felt they were unable to help Mrs Rogers with the remainder required but due to 'her excellent character as an industrious woman' the Vestry meeting sanctioned her approaching parishioners who may help. Mrs Rogers was successful as the Vestry minutes of 19 April 1854 record that Mr Thomas Armstrong had no objection to going to London to see Sarah Rogers properly started.

The mid 19th century saw an outbreak of typhoid sweep through the inhabitants. In the autumn of 1846, a special Vestry meeting was convened 'to consider the best means for aiding and relieving the suffering poor in the parish at the present crisis' after recording that it was typhus of a most virulent form. There and then the people in the room collected £10 7 shillings 6 pence to procure beef, wine, sheets, chloride of lime and other articles necessary. Before the outbreak abated early into the following year 31 people had died from a population of around 750, many of them children and teenagers. Many families were affected including Kendall, Cooper, Toll, Sharp, Burr and Masters.

> **DID YOU KNOW?**
> Henry VIII and Elizabeth I both passed acts to allow for the killing of vermin. The 1566 statute in particular fixed the price for a hedgehog at 2d each. Although common in many parishes, not a single mention is made of payments for hedgehogs in Wilstead. When a later Georgian statute made amendment so that payments would be made if the vermin was 'kylde and taken within their parisshe' the churchwardens account books show payments for 20 pole cats, 4 foxes, 5 badgers and 6,600 sparrows.

Reaching the end of the second millennium brings us into the recollections and facts of the 20th century. Many of these are recorded elsewhere in this book but it would be remiss to close without including a few poignant moments.

The first military wedding for the parish took place at All Saints in November 1915 when Miss Martha Berrington married Sergeant Foster of the Royal Engineers stationed at Haynes Park. Their wedding breakfast was held in the clubroom of the Elephant and Castle.

The first interment of cremated remains in the churchyard was carried out in January 1916 when the casket of Mary Harriett Fowler was interred in the tomb of her father, Sir William Morgan, K.C.M.G.

In 1965, the television cameras of Anglia Television came to film and talk to Mr Frederick Bennett, a well known villager. Mr Bennett had been the landlord in the

original Red Lion public house (now a private property) as well as being a bricklay-
er who specialised in Church work. In 1965, he was nominated for being the oldest
newspaper rounds man at the age of 82 when he delivered papers for his daughter
Doris Croot, who kept the post office.

A final second millennium moment is captured in the following 1990s poem.

The Wilshamstead Village Post Office

For service and civility the place is hard to beat
It's organised, efficient, orderly and neat
It's the fulcrum of the village, where people like to meet
To buy a stamp, or birthday card, perchance a friend to greet.

Derek stands behind the grille, large as life is he,
Serious, unsmiling – he's been up since half past three!
Dispensing morning papers – his early morning chore
Ensures correct deliveries through each and every door.

See nearby, his able staff, bedecked in Arsenal red,
Providing, oh so many things, from shoelaces to bread,
Sweets and meats and sealing wax, even pairs of socks
Amazing what's available from vast and varied stocks.

They work with smooth efficiency, serving this and that
And yet it seems they're not averse to have a little chat.
"Good morning, Mrs Pickering, How was your holiday?
Weather to your liking? Did you enjoy your stay?
Here's that first class stamp required to post your urgent letter.
Morning Mabel, trust you're well, is Harry any better?"

Defying all the elements like rain and wind or hail
Four stalwart ladies pedal forth delivering our mail.
Regular as clockwork, hardly ever late
A service and amenity we all appreciate.

Now some collect their papers each morning without fail
The 'thinking' ones, they have 'The Sun' - others have 'The Mail'
Or 'Telegraph' or 'Guardian', 'The Times' of course and such
A pleasant way to start the day with just the human touch.

We all discuss the weather, we grumble or extol
Janet flits upon the scene, quiet but in control,
For there is something special here, a sort of an allure
That isn't found in Sainsburys' nor Tescos', that's for sure!
And should we ever come to lose this prized facility
Then you and me and village life will so much poorer be.

Jim McCarthy

CHAPTER 7

Crime and Punishment

Crime and wrong doing may not be the original sin but misdemeanours have always formed a large part in local history. Wilstead has its own stories and we recount some of them in these pages to show how times and punishments have changed.

Most people have heard of punishment in the stocks as they proved to be a successful form of punishment in which criminals were exposed to public ridicule and assault. Wilstead had its own pair of stocks and although no evidence can be found of their location, it is probable they were near to the crossroads possibly on the village green. There is evidence that they were in use in the mid 18th century, as a new set was paid for in 1769 at the cost of 15 shillings and 3 pence. In 1792 there is a record of a further 1 shilling nine pence being paid to John Tuffnail for 'ironwork at the stocks and a lock'. The Tuffnail family were the black-smiths at this time at the nearby smithy and they would have been able to provide these metal parts. Still in use in 1830, the stocks held William Yoxon and Samuel Penwright for four hours when they failed to make payment on a fine that had been imposed on them for being drunk and making a disturbance in church. As it is a pair of stocks and two people seemed to have been restrained at the same time, it is

Stocks at Chapel-en-le-Frith

(copyright: buxtononline.net2002)

possible that our village stocks looked something similar to a pair of stocks that still exist in Chapel - En -Le-Frith in Derbyshire.

The nineteenth century was a hard time. The introduction of the Corn Laws in 1815 and other changing aspects of agricultural production caused considerable agitation as food prices rose. Feelings often ran high and inter-village feeling was strong. At a disturbance in 1826 between Wilstead people and those from Haynes, Wilstonians shouted that ' they would not go while all [until] Haynes people had left the field, they would not be drove'.

Villagers helped to support themselves by growing their own food and so the theft of beehives in 1819 was a serious offence.

Elizabeth Bull's father was a grazier in the village and he also kept bees in his garden. One day Elizabeth missed two of their ten hives but after searching with their servant Richard Thompson, they found the missing hives in the field adjoining the garden. One hive had been cut open and the honey taken out, the other hive containing the honey of both, had been hidden in the hedge. After reporting it, Thomas Crozeley the constable, Richard Thompson, the servant, Abraham Burr (baker), William Izzard (labourer), James Green (labourer) and Thomas Dines were set to watch the hives.

About 11pm, two men came walking along the hedge side. One of them, John Cranfield, was wearing a long smock frock. He stepped over the ditch and hung over the hedge to reach the honey. The other man who was wearing a short smock frock stood close by. His name was John Arnold. As Cranfield took hold of the hive with the honey, Thomas Crozeley, the constable, jumped up and said 'so you have come for it but you shall not have it'. Cranfield and Arnold both then reached under their smock frocks and took out two heavy sticks. Damning the watchers blood and pronouncing they were ready for them, Arnold and Cranfield said they would either kill or be killed.

Thomas Crozeley, the constable, received several severe and heavy blows on the shoulder, on the jaw and one on the mouth. Warning Cranfield that he would shoot him if he struck anymore, he used the pistol to ward off the blows. Cranfield struck him one last time on the temple before running off with Arnold. Thomas Dines who was nearby called out for assistance but as he did so the culprits struck out at the men coming to help including William Izzard. Arnold struck James Green with a stick but Green managed to hit back with his bill hook before Arnold tried to throttle him.

At this point Thomas Crozeley fired his pistols at the prisoners and wounded Cranfield in the back of his leg and thigh having shot at their legs.

Arnold and Cranfield turned and went back to Crozeley with Arnold striking Crozeley in the face with his fist. He had successfully cut Abraham Burr's lip with a similar fist punch in the earlier scuffle.

The men were then all involved in another scuffle and after 45 minutes the prisoners were finally secured. Thinking they would have their freedom some time soon, the prisoners both swore that they would kill all of the watchers as soon as they got their liberty. They claimed they had not come for the honey but for a spree as they had heard that people were watching the bees.

Once in custody in the public house, the two men denied they knew anything about the honey but had been going to see their sweethearts in Houghton Conquest. At the trial on 9 October 1819 both John Arnold aged 18 and John

Cranfield aged 20 were found guilty and were sentenced to seven years transportation and penal servitude for stealing bees and honey. They were delivered on board the prison hulk Justitia on 3 November 1819.

It is likely that the public house mentioned in the case of Arnold and Cranfield was the original Red Lion public house, which was often used for cases by constables. The original pub is now a private property and is set back from the later public house that bears the same name and is still in operation today.

The original public house establishment was the setting for a public disturbance crime in 1830. Elizabeth Toll summoned William Whittamore, a farmer and one of the parish constables, to put a stop to a disturbance outside Bennett's house. Bennett was the landlord of the Red Lion and on that day he had started to sell ale under a new act.

At this time the village green extended up to the property and a small field (or close) was adjacent. More than 100 people were in the close making a disturbance whilst two men, Joseph Pearce and Benjamin Titmus, were stripped to the skin and fighting by lantern light.

When William Whittamore gave evidence he said he had called out that there must be no more fighting but some of the crowd had cried back that they would not be stopped by any constable. Francis Ambridge then struck the constable on the head and swore the fight would not be stopped before striking Whittamore several more times. The constable retaliated before he was again struck on the head, this time by Joseph Pearce, one of the fighters. The mob then overwhelmed the constable, beating him very badly. He later said he hadn't expected to get up alive. Calling out MURDER, he at last got up and called for assistance and was aided by Mr Burr, Mr Quimby and Joseph Dines. Warrants were later issued for the arrest of Francis Ambridge and Joseph Pearce and they were bound over to keep the peace. William Whittamore, the constable, was so badly injured that he had to pay a man for five weeks to look after his farm.

Disagreements in the villages of Cardington, Cotton End, Lidlington and Wilshamstead between farmers and agricultural labourers over a 2 shilling rise brought the president of the national agricultural labourers union to Bedford where speeches were made and the disagreement discussed. This local episode clearly reflected the national feeling, which was made famous by the transportation of the Tolpuddle Martyrs in Dorset for swearing an oath to an illegal labourers union.

The issue of pay for agricultural workers is one of the popular strands in the story of local lad, James Addington.

The well known local tale is that of a boy who was hung for setting fire to a haystack because he received less pay than other boys his age. Unfortunately popularisation of this story, both in books and in it's telling, has over time left out many of the true facts. James Addington was not a victim of circumstance, as the tale would lead us to believe and the true account of why he was hung is very much different.

Addington's first appearance before the court came in 1830 following an affray.

Demanding food from the workhouse master along with his friend, Richard Ambridge, Addington had shouted 'there are plenty of victuals here and we will have some raw or cooked'. The Wilstead workhouse wasn't a large affair but small and managed part time by notables from the village. The workhouse master involved in this incident was William Whittamore who was the parish constable and a farmer and who had been involved in the disturbance outside the Red Lion.

Once he had confirmed that the parish overseer had not sent the boys to the workhouse for food, Whittamore struggled with them to put them back outside. As the struggle continued he called for his constable's staff and it is reported that this annoyed Addington so that he threatened 'I'll go to hell, if I don't let your guts out if you offer to touch me with that staff'.

When the matter of the affray came up in court, Addington was sentenced to enter into recognisance with his father to keep the peace.

The following year in January 1831, it was reported that Addington had set fire to a hayrick belonging to Thomas Dines, farmer and assistant parish overseer. As the hayrick had value, Farmer Dines was keen to see guilt placed and because the hayrick was in an open place and reputedly a favourite haunt of Addington's, it was easy to place blame on the boy.

The local story says Addington set fire to the rick because Mr Dines paid him six-pence less a week than other boys and it was for this he was hung. However, in reality, the quarter sessions court in March 1831, which dealt with this arson charge, acquitted the boy of the crime. During the trail though a point was made of describing how Addington's conduct in gaol whilst awaiting trial had been badly disposed.

Unfortunately, the behaviour of Addington did not improve. By November 1831 he was once again in gaol on three serious charges. The first two were housebreaking, during one of which a gun was stolen. The third charge was again arson with James Addington being charged with setting fire to a barn on Friday 11 November 1831 in the evening. The barn was once again the property of Thomas Dines and his tenement was located where Dines Close is today.

Manor House (Date of photograph unknown although believed to be early 20th century)

(Reproduced with the kind permission of Sylvia Bowen)

The *Bedfordshire Express* reported on the trial of James Addington, which took place at Bedford Assizes in 1832. From their detailed accounts we can follow the details of the event.

James Addington, who was 18, had left his work at the farm of Mr Armstrong in the company of his friend George Rogers a younger boy aged about 12. William Armstrong, was farming at Manor Farm. Addington gave Rogers money and sent him to buy a half ounce of tobacco from Morgan's shop whilst he walked on. The Morgan family resided in the large property now known as Manor House and were grocers.

Reaching the house of Francis Ambridge which was approximately 70 yards from Thomas Dines barn, Addington asked for a light for his pipe. Ambridge asked the lad how long he had been a smoker as he hadn't known him to smoke before and Addington replied he had been a smoker for a long time. Lighting his pipe he smoked it partly out before leaving the house at a quarter to eight. Ambridge testified that it was about 10 minutes after Addington had left when he heard the alarm of fire.

In the meantime, Addington had made his way to the Black Hat public house. George Morgan who was already in the public house informed the trial that when Addington arrived just before 8 o'clock he had no pipe. Morgan stated it was only a short time after Addington's arrival before the alarm of fire was heard. Morgan, Addington and a Mr Spring rushed out to the fire and Joseph Redman later testified that Addington had helped put the fire out.

Mary Phillips, landlady of the Black Hat Public House noticed that when Addington returned to the pub at 2am, he appeared greatly confused and when other people in the pub exclaimed 'that the person who caused it ought to be burned or hanged' he became agitated and 'walked around the house'.

Two days later on the Sunday, Addington walked past the site once more in the company of his young friend George Rogers. Addington intimated that the farmers were after him for the burning of the barn because he had previously set fire to the haystack. Addington had previously been acquitted of this earlier crime and regretting that he had made this verbal admission he asked Rogers not to tell anyone. Sometime later George Rogers told his father what Addington had confided to him and Addington was apprehended

When the trial began, Addington's defence was that he had not caused the fire but that a Thomas Sharpe had committed the deed. He said he had lit his pipe at Polly Child's house when Sharpe had walked by and asked for a smoke. Together they had walked towards Dines's barn whereupon Sharpe had gone into the yard and Addington thought Sharpe took tobacco out of his pipe and put it into the side of the barn.

Sharpe was the principle prosecution witness. He also worked for Mr Armstrong and testified that after both he and Addington had been scolded for not doing their work by Mr Armstrong on 21 November 1831 (ten days after the fire) that Addington had said 'I can trust you with a secret. I went to Polly Child's house to light my pipe and I went to Dines's and it was done'. Sharpe apparently asked

Addington if he had been alone and Addington had told him he had been.

The trial took an unusual turn at this point as witnesses were called to try to discredit Thomas Sharpe. An example of this was Thomas Stokes who testified that when he had been transported to Bermuda for seven years, Thomas Sharpe was already there as a convict using the name of John Glover.

Mary Burn however was Thomas Sharpe's landlady and she told the trial how Sharpe had gone to bed at 6 o Clock the evening of the fire and only got up when the alarm was given.

The trial lasted for four hours. The charges of housebreaking and burglary were dropped but a guilty verdict was returned against Addington on the arson charge.

The *Bedfordshire Express* reported that at the end of the trial, Addington shed tears and said just once ' It was Thomas Sharpe who did it'. The quarter sessions sentenced him to be executed.

During his time in Bedford Gaol awaiting execution, Addington is reputed to have carved a hare onto a piece of wood. Many people in the village today recall this achievement as for years the hare hung on the wall at the smithy at the cross-roads. The workers preserved it by wiping paint from their brushes onto it. The hare picture still exists and although no longer in the village it remains in the possession of the Mastin family who had owned the smithy.

Shortly after James Addington's conviction, it is reported that he made a full confession to Reverend Maclear the gaol chaplain to starting the fire at the barn and the haystack. When asked for his motive he failed to give a reply but did say it wasn't from malice towards Mr Dines.

A later report says he confessed that his motive had been due to aggrievement that Mr Dines as overseer had paid him sixpence less a week than some of his fellow labourers but this had not been raised before.

The hanging of James Addington took place on 24 March 1832 on the flat roof of the turnkeys lodge at the entrance to Bedford Gaol.

Although convicted of arson, the book from Bedford gaol records the event simply:

YEAR	NAME	AGE	NATURE OF OFFENCE COMMITTED	DATE OF EXECUTION
1832	Addington James	18	House Breaking	March 24 1832

The hanging took place on the day of the Bedford market and a Bedford school-boy who later became the famous judge Lord Brampton, described the transportation of Addington's body from the gaol. He had a vantage point in an upper schoolroom in the Bedford school house on the side of St Paul's Square facing the high street. From the reminiscences of Sir Henry Hawkins, Lord Brampton, Vol 1 pp 2–4:

'Suddenly a great silence came over the people and a sudden gloom that made a great despondency in my mind without my knowing why. Public solemnity affects even the youngest of us, at all events it affected me. Presently – and deeply is the event impressed on my mind after seventy years of busy life – I saw emerging from a by street that led from Bedford gaol and coming along the square and near the window where I was standing, a common cart, drawn by a horse which was led by a labouring man. As I was above the crowd on the first floor, I could see there was a layer of straw in the cart at the bottom and above it, tumbled in a rough heap as though carelessly thrown in, a quantity of the same; and I could see also from the surrounding circumstances especially the pallid faces of the crowd, that there was something sad about it all. The horse moved slowly along, at almost snails pace while behind walked a poor sad couple with their heads bowed down and each with a hand on the tail board of the cart. They were evidently overwhelmed with grief......the cart contained the rude shell into which had been laid the body of a poor man and woman's only son, a youth of seventeen, hanged that morning at Bedford gaol for setting fire to a stack of corn. He was being conveyed to the village of Wilshamstead six miles from Bedford, there to be laid in the churchyard where in his childhood he had played.'

A day after the hanging, James Addington was interred at All Saints, Wilstead and recorded in the parishes registers as below. The grave location is unknown and unmarked.

NAME	ABODE	When Buried	AGE	By whom the ceremony was performed
James Addington	Wilstead	March 25th 1832	18 years	F Pawsey

On the very same day that James Addington was hanged another young Wilstead man was sentenced in court. William Clarke, aged 21 and described as being 5 feet 4 inches tall with dark hair and a dark complexion was found guilty of stealing flour. Like Arnold and Cranfield 18 years earlier, William Clarke was sentenced to 7 years transportation and penal servitude. He was delivered to the prison hulk Justitia on 14 April 1832.

Whilst crime and wrong doings take place in all parishes, the place of custody of the prisoner is rarely recorded before they are taken to the prisons. Wilstead however, had its own lock up or cage. Cages were used before the establishment of a county police force and the parish was responsible for law and order within its own boundaries.

It has not been possible to establish when the cage was erected but it is possible that Richard Green of Sundon who was 'kept in custody' at Wilstead in 1812 was placed in the cage. The parish received 6 shillings for providing this assistance. In 1857 the 19th March Vestry minutes record that ' it was unanimously resolved that the cage have a new iron roof on' . Much later, a reminiscence of Mr H B Sharpe, recorded in 1962, recalls that around 1900, traces were left of the cage by its shape in the plaster on the outside of the Church House by the church yard gates. This recollection is substantiated by Reverend Whitworth who wrote in 1904 that the cage had been annexed to the northern wall of the west end of Church House. Reverend Whitworth records that it hadn't been many years since the cage had been demolished and that the only remaining sign was the outline of the pitch of the roof against the front wall of the cottage. He described it as 'a receptacle for the temporary detention of the inhabitant whose dissolute or dishonest conduct threatened public peace and security'.

All the events in this chapter would have been witnessed by George Rogers. Born in 1819, he lived his entire life in Wilstead and was the first postman and then a well known carrier. In the tale of James Addington, George Rogers is mentioned and it is likely this is the same person. George liked to write acrostics and shared his verses with the village. The following verses about the Thomas Phipps grocers shop were written by George Rogers in a time contemporary to many of the events listed in this chapter.

Teas of the best and cheapest kind
Hams, eggs and Bacon too
Old Cheshire Cheese rich as you please
Mixed pickles, starch and blue

All sorts of spices, whole and ground
Soap – brown and mottled too
Pepper and mustard. Scented snuff
Hogs lard and treacle too

In jars – preserves of every kind
Plums, damson and likewise
Plaid dresses too both red and blue
Such as will please your eyes

Good drapery you here can buy
Right as in larger towns
Or if you please you there can buy
Cotton or wollen gowns

Each article you purchase here
Right good you will always find
Weight, quality and moderate price
Is always kept in mind

Likewise he sells all kinds of nails
Spikes, tacks and London clouts
The very best that Birmingham
Ever did turn out

And if you wish the truth to know
Direct to T Phipps shop you should go

CHAPTER 8

Chapels and Churches

Other than All Saints church, Wilshamstead has been the home for Methodism, Evangelism and a second Anglican church.

METHODISM

Methodism was introduced into the village by William Armstrong of Manor Farm. By donating land and money he enabled the first Wesleyan Chapel to be built on the right hand side of Chapel Lane in 1808. In 1841, on the same site he laid the foundation stone of a new larger chapel.

This later Wesleyan Chapel was constructed of brick and slate. The central doorway was an ornamental rectangular column and the Chapel had sash windows on the ground and first floor. The sidewalls were of red brick and there was a gallery to the rear of the building.

The Wesleyan Methodist Chapel was formed by an indenture of 1854

Wesleyan Chapel (of 1841)

(Reproduced with the kind permission of Miriam Langford)

and was regulated by the Schemes of the Charities Commissioners of 1871.

William Armstrong was a member and leader of the Wesleyan Society for almost 40 years. He died on 28 July 1845, aged 76 years, and left a large estate valued at £3000. Both William and his wife Mary were buried at the chapel, but nothing has ever been found of their graves except their daughter's headstone, Mary Anne who died in 1825, at 19 years of age.

William and Mary Armstrong.
(Reproduced with kind permission of Jim Armstrong)

Following the introduction of beer houses and reduced beer prices came the start of the temperance movement and in 1847 Wilstead Chapel founded its Band of Hope. Its aim was to discourage the drinking of spirits and liquor. Songs such as 'drink water from the crystal stream' reflect this idea and speakers presenting a magic lantern show would describe the unhappiness of those children whose father spent the family income on beer.

The Band of Hope lasted for many years and it was the custom up until the 1920s for the Wilstead Band of Hope to hold an annual summer parade. The people would carry a blue banner and sing along the way from the chapel to the village crossroads. A tea and evensong would then follow in the chapel. In 1862 the local paper reported:

> On Whit-Tuesday the village was aroused from its accustomed quiet by the youthful members of the Band of Hope marching in procession and singing their temperance songs, on their way to the grounds of Mr Thomas Newman. A plentiful supply of tea and cake was provided for the little ones. In the evening a large meeting was held.

Band of Hope

(Reproduced with the kind permission of Miriam Langford)

The Chapel acted as the centre of many early village activities. The Rechabite Friendly Society in Wilstead held meetings in the Chapel and records show that the caretaker was paid 3 shillings 9 pence a week for cleaning and to ensure that the stoves were lighted to provide heating. In addition to the weekly Band of Hope and Prayer meetings there was a weekly Sunday school.

During the First World War, soldiers from Haynes camp marched to the Wesleyan Chapel on a Sunday morning sometimes bringing their own preacher. The Chapel would be so full that some people had to go into the gallery.

Music was provided by a Trustam, a hand operated pipe organ. This was so old that the organ blower, Mr Barden, found it difficult to get enough wind in the bellows to keep it going and so a small organ had to be used for the services.

To replace the large organ, Mr Irons, the deputy organ blower, found a sale advertisement for an organ 150 years old. After inspection, the Reverend Allan Harling and the trustees arranged for its purchase from Gorton Parish Church in Manchester for £150. Plans were made for its transportation to Wilstead.

In the autumn of 1949, it took a total of 12 men to dismantle the organ. Mr Steele was the main person responsible for the dismantling and rebuilding of the organ and 2 lorries were needed to bring it home.

Approximately, 10.000 pieces of the organ had to be labelled before they could be transported and these were laid out in the pews. It took 7 men to load the pieces and console. When it arrived at Wilshamstead, the 1,522 organ pipes had to be stored in the church vestry whilst the services were held in the schoolroom which was located on the left-hand side of the chapel.

The vestry ceiling then had to be removed to allow for the tall organ pipes. A pit of four feet was dug for brick pier to hold the east wall and cracks were filled in to prevent the bricks falling. As it was gradually built up the old vestry wall was carefully removed.

The majority of the organ was assembled in the vestry, with the various lengths of lead pipes being soldered into their sockets. The organ was placed cornerwise on the east side of the chapel. A tablet was fixed on the chapel wall and members gave donations to have their relatives' names recorded as a memory to mark the installation of the organ.

The official opening ceremony took place on 27th May 1950. A full history of the organ was compiled by Mr Ralph Cooper and can be found in the records office.

This chapel had served the community for over 125 years but unfortunately when the ceiling fell down after the christening of 2 babies, the trustees were faced with high costs of repairs and the need to replace the floors and pews.

A decision had to be made and enquiries were made. This led to a new site on the edge of a new housing estate site on Cotton End Road. Mr Cyril Taylor from Ivy Lane provided the land for the church to be built on.

In 1966 the plans for a new church were completed by the architects, E H C Inskip & Son of Goldington Road, Bedford. Under the guidance of the Minister at the time, Rev Frederick Pilkington, plans were also made to demolish the 125-year-old chapel in Chapel Lane.

On 21st April 1967 two of the longest serving chapel members laid the foundation stone. Mrs Gladys Tucker of Ampthill smoothed the mortar and then 88 year old Mrs Sarah Mastin of Wilstead, tapped the foundation stone in place. The open-air ceremony took place in a wind swept field, as the houses had not yet been built.

The new Methodist church was completed at a cost of approximately £22,000 with the organ move costing £1,800.

A tablet to the memory of William and Mary Armstrong was transferred from the old chapel to the new Methodist church and is located on the wall in the entrance today.

THE MISSION HALL – EVANGELICAL CHURCH

The Mission Hall was founded in 1894 when a number of people met together for Christian worship and called themselves Primitive Methodists. They purchased the site of a cottage previously owned by Job Kingham in Cotton End Road. Charles Smith of Wilshamstead acting as trustee registered it on 17 April 1895.

TRUSTEES	
Benjamin Billington	John Savage
Isaac Brightman	Frederick Simms
William Grooms	Alfred Smith
Thomas Izzard	Charles Smith
James Potter	Thomas Smith
Thomas Richardson	

The trustees made arrangements to clear the site and construct a building of galvanised corrugated iron.

One of the founders was Mr Benjamin Billington who was born at Haynes on 1st August 1846. He spent most of his life in the Bedfordshire area working as a brickyard labourer and then in Wilshamstead as a farm labourer at Duck End Farm. A relative of Benjamin has memories of visiting Benjamin in his cottage at 5 Duck End Lane during the summer holidays and recalls seeing and hearing Benjamin saying his prayers by his bedside.

Benjamin married Ann Grooms on 10th January 1873 and had 3 daughters: Kate, Ellen and Clara. Research has shown that Ellen married in 1898 at All Saints Parish Church because the Wilshamstead Mission did not have a licence for the Solemnisation of Matrimony. Ann Grooms was a talented lace maker and she

Early Mission Hall made of corrugated iron
(Reproduced with the kind permission of Miriam Langford)

Early photograph of 5 Duck End Lane
(Reproduced with kind permission of Adam Raine)

helped to provide for the family's income by selling her lace in Bedford. Benjamin and Ann lived at 5 Duck End Lane in Wilshamstead, which is one of three cottages still standing today.

In the early 1900s music was provided at the Mission Hall by Walter Cooper, the organist, Arthur Cooper on the bass and Frank Cooper with the violin.

In 1954 the original iron building was replaced with brick walls and a tiled roof. The Mission Hall was renamed in the late 1980s to Wilstead Evangelical Church and it is affiliated to the Fellowship of Independent Evangelical Churches.

ST PAULS CHURCH

In the 19th century, the Anglican Church decided it was necessary to provide a place of worship for Littleworth and Potter's End villagers. Although the idea was conceived around 1870, in reality it did not start taking shape until 1898. St Paul's Church stood prominently on the corner at Littleworth. Today, there are no signs or remains to show that this little church once existed except for a new house, which stands on the same site displaying a plaque which reads St Paul's MCM-LXXXI (1981).

To many people, the church was commonly known as the 'little tin church', the nickname being derived from its construction of corrugated iron. Other nicknames included 'tin tang tabernacle' and 'the pink church'. It had been painted with red oxide on the corrugated iron.

By January 1899 the first funds were received and in 1900 a fund called the 'Church room fund at Littleworth' had been set up and several contributions had been received from the Littleworth Mothers' Meeting.

It wasn't until 1905 that sufficient monies were raised to enable the building operations to begin and the land to be purchased from Mr B Cambers. A building of stone or brick was considered at the time but as the subscriptions received were too sparse, it was decided to build it of cheaper materials. In November 1905 the contractor, Mr William Harbrow of South Bermondsey was made responsible for the work.

The church interior measured 54 ft in length by 20 ft in breadth and provided a capacity for approximately 130 people. It consisted of a chancel, a vestry and a porch. To prevent damp, the floor and wall foundations were lined with a bed of concrete and layers of felt were placed in between the wood and iron work of the roof. The opening ceremony was originally intended for 25th January 1906, St Paul's Day, but this proved not to be possible.

St Paul's Church Littleworth

(Reproduced with the kind permission of
Dorothy Houghton)

Interior of St Paul's

(Reproduced with the kind permission of
Dorothy Houghton)

Although the church was still dedicated in the name of St Paul, the ceremony finally took place on 27th February 1906 and it was conducted by the Canon Macauley, a former vicar of the village. Both Canon Macaulay and his wife showed great affection for the parish. In 1916 Mrs Macaulay, presented several gifts to St Paul's church, some of which had been made by Mrs Macaulay herself. They included a solid silver chalice and paten cruet with silver top, a brass altar desk, a service book, a chalice veil, and a purple altar frontal.

Although licensed by the Bishop for divine service it was not consecrated, which meant it could also be used for social functions. Initially, the church did not have a licence to marry and all marriages were held at All Saints Parish Church but in later years the church gained its licence and the first wedding was of Phyllis Summerfield of Wilstead and L Hoy of Luton in Autumn 1935.

Various feasts were observed at St Paul's including the feast of St Michael and All Angels. The lesson would be read to the congregation followed by an evensong and a procession arranged by the Master of Ceremonies. The feast of Whitsun was concluded with a procession represented by members of the Guild bearing lights and on Palm Sunday palms were distributed, followed by a procession through Littleworth.

*The Servers of St Paul's
painting the exterior
of the church – May 1937,
which appeared in the local paper.*

*(Reproduced with kind permission
of Rose Summerfield)*

*Mr Douglas Wolveridge
with choirboys.*

*(Reproduced with the kind permission
of Rose Summerfield)*

St Paul's church room was regularly used for socials and dances organised by the parents of the children of the Catechism classes. These included Christmas tea parties, and without fail Santa Claus made a surprise visit to distribute the presents! By 1935 there were as many as 70 children in the Church Catechism Classes. Jumble sales were also held there in aid of the Nursing Association. St Paul's Church Room was frequently used for 'lantern' lectures and guest speakers spoke about various topics such as 'Historical Bedfordshire' and the funds went towards the Catechism Children's Christmas Fund.

St Paul's is mostly associated with Mr Douglas Wolveridge, known as Dougie, he was the lay preacher or reader at the Littleworth church. He was deeply involved with many village activities as well as organising and writing plays for the children to act in the church. He was also active in fundraising such as Buttercup Day, which collected monies for the church by the sale of posies of buttercups by girls.

As the congregation diminished in number the church slowly fell out of use and was demolished in the 1950s.

CHAPTER 9

The Social Circle

Wilshamstead has always been renowned as a busy village with many social activities to suit all ages. An early parish magazine once captured this by saying 'Wilstead entertainments have acquired a reputation beyond the limits of our village'.

The earliest reference is a musician living in the village in the 17th century. Prior to this, the opportunity of hearing music was rare and was mainly only available to the populace at church services.

At the turn of the 20th century, the vicarage encouraged a social life uniting the people and community in social gatherings. Many groups of this period organised their social meetings and entertainment here including knitting classes, Sunday school festivals and the women's class enjoying teas, followed by music, dancing and all kinds of games.

The Vicarage also hosted a number of celebrations including the Christmas teas of the Uptown (main body of the village) Mothers Meeting group and festivities

Mothers Union at vicarage (unknown date)

(Reproduced with the kind permission of Brian Crouch)

for the Littleworth Mothers Group. The Mother's Union today is as active as it was a century ago and in August 2001 it commemorated the 125th Anniversary of its founding.

As the number of church helpers increased over the years the parties for them moved to the National schoolroom. The evening party consisted of dancing, singing and playing games. Mrs Whitworth was the leading spirit at such events and music was provided by the playing of an organette and the piano. She was highly regarded and in January 1901 the village presented her with a silver-plated egg stand 'as a small token of esteem'.

The choral society practised in the rooms and occasionally the bible class and choral society would present a service of song at the church. The choral society's annual summer trip was usually to the seaside but occasionally, when the crops matured early and it was necessary to undertake the harvest, the trips were postponed to September.

The services for Harvest Festival would be held at 8am, 10am and 7pm. The Sunday afternoon would see a public tea and jumble sale in the Vicarage garden. The Harvest Festival continues to be celebrated today with a special service at the parish church for parents and children of the village lower school. Gifts of food are currently donated to the Christian Family Care Centre in Bedford.

Reverend Whitworth occasionally organised evenings of cinematography. The first one was held on 19th April 1900 and provided the villagers with a new experience. Many had never before witnessed the art of photography and the photographs shown were from the South African war or of a comic nature. Proceeds from these events were forwarded to the Mansion House Transvaal War Fund that supported the widows and orphans of soldiers and sailors.

Entertainment was also provided in the form of concerts and garden parties at the Vicarage. Local performers sang popular songs such as: 'The Old Brigade', 'Our Jack's come home today', 'Ambulance Maids' and the 'Lads in Navy Blue'. This continued for many years. On 1st September 1934 the admission fee to the 'Wilshamstead Vicarage Concert and Garden Party' was advertised at 6d. During the 1950s parties, people would congregate on the lawn after a Sunday evening service and Bedford Town Silver Band would play.

Vicarage fetes were organised by the vicar and parochial council and this has been a tradition that has grown from strength to strength over the decades. Originally, the annual church fetes took place on the vicarage lawn but in modern times they have moved to the church interior. The All Saints fete of the millennium year 2000 included Mr Seamark carrying out a display with geese and sheepdogs and the Brownies entertained the locals with their singing.

Fetes were held by the Methodist Chapel as well. In the 1930s these were held annually on the field in Chapel Close which was owned by the Mastin family who were part of the congregation. This field was to the west of Chapel Lane and the family allowed use of their tennis court and mini golf course. Modern housing now occupies the site.

Many modern villagers recall the Wilshamstead street parties of Queen

Chapel Close Fete 1930s

(Reproduced with the kind permission of Hilda Bourne)

Elizabeth II Silver Jubilee in 1977 but this was an already established tradition.

The Silver Jubilee of King George V and Queen Mary in 1935 was commemorated by a big outdoor party in the field next to the infant school. A parade of members of the British Legion, the Women's Institute, Scouts, Girl Guides and Brownies marched to the parish church where a special service of thanksgiving was conducted by the Reverend Harry Pollard. A similar event took place in the evening at St Paul's Littleworth.

On 12 May 1937, a fancy dress parade was held to celebrate the Coronation of King George VI. Mugs and spoons were distributed to the children and a fete was held in the British Legion Hut.

In 1952 similar celebrations were held to commemorate the coronation of Queen Elizabeth II. This time a fancy dress party for the children was held in the village hall. Street parties were organised by residents.

For the Queen's Coronation the village also prepared a float on the back of a trailer, and the theme it centred on was 'Bridge Sports Salutes the Queen'. The float had people dressed up as footballers, cricketers and a small group were seated around a table playing cards as representatives of the 'Old Sports'.

Floats formed a large part of the Bedford Carnival, which is now known as the River Festival. Wilshamstead's entries began in 1975 when the Parish Council approached the Wilstead Players to enter a float. A committee was formed and the founder members were Gordon Maskell and family, Derek Smith, Ray Terry, Rosemary Boston, Ron Ashton, Ella Ashton, Rick Baxter and Jane Wooding.

The floats were a group effort and were always built on Gordon Maskell's flat bed lorry in his farmyard at Duck End. Scrap materials and timber frames were mainly used in the process but the Parish Council contributed towards the cost of any other materials, whilst the local school children, committee members and Wilstead players helped with the costumes.

The first float in May 1975 portrayed an Ali Baba theme. It won the Cup for 'First in Class'. In July 1977 Wilshamstead presented the Old English Village float which won both the Cup for First in Class and the Challenge Cup. Other prizes were won for the theme entries of Tales of the Riverbank in May 1978, Alice in Wonderland in May 1980 and Peter Pan in May 1984.

In the 1990 festival, Wilshamstead presented the Wizard of Oz float and won the 'Best float entered by a village' as well as the 'First in Class Cup'. The rainbow

Wizard of Oz float 1990

(Reproduced with the kind permission of Ray Terry)

consisted of a plastic pole with 18 inches drop of white net curtains that had been sprayed in all the colours. The last entry was made in May 1994 with a Nursery Rhyme float.

For many years a major social occasion in the village was the annual 'Stati' fair. Visiting travelling fairs began in the medieval period with merchants and entertainers, jugglers and musicians arriving. When the Black Death decreased the working population and created a shortage of labourers and servants, the national Statute of Labourers of 1351 was introduced. Statute fairs then became a means by which employers could find suitable labour. Over the centuries the event evolved into amusement fairs. For Wilshamstead, this meant being visited annually by a travelling fair such as the Mannings. The name 'stati' is derived from the original 'statute'. The first roundabouts were in the early 18th century and originally propelled by a gang of boys but by 1868 they were driven by steam. Later came the steam operated 'galloping horses' remembered by several villagers.

The stati fair was held in the field between the original Red Lion Public House and the Black Hat Public House on part of the village green. Later, when the green was developed, the fair moved to a field adjacent to The Rose Public House in Littleworth.

A stall sold Stati Rock, which was locally known as Spit Rock. It was a triangular rock with brown and white stripes. Apparently so called because the maker would spit on his or her hands so that the rock could be rolled more easily! Despite the method used we have been assured it tasted delicious. In the 1940s people looked forward to eating the Stati Rock to the sound of Guy Mitchell's songs when the music could be heard all over the village. The travelling fairs stopped visiting the village sometime in the 1950s but they can still be found today in Bedford.

In the 1960s a ladies group was formed by Veronica Scargill which included reading plays together and a Young Wives group was started up by Enid Wisson. The ladies met on an informal basis arranging guest speakers regularly. Wilstead Pre-school Playgroup has its origins in a meeting of the Young Wives held in 1967 and it still operates today in the village hall in Cotton End Road.

The active Young Wives group went on to create the Keep Fit Group and Meals on Wheels Group and with Enid Wisson beginning a Get to know your Neighbour Campaign there was a welcome for young mothers who had recently moved into the village. Unfortunately, many of these groups have ceased although many members of the Young Wives went on to join the Women's Institute.

The Women's Institute in Wilshamstead was formed in 1931 with funds of one guinea. A committee was elected with Mrs Crawley as President and Mrs Hughes and Miss Hilda Cox as Vice Presidents, Miss Toll as Secretary and Mrs Brewster as Treasurer. Meetings were held in the Parish Room inside the vicarage and opened with the song Jerusalem. The meetings were closed with the national anthem. One of the first outings was a visit to Frean's Chocolate Factory.

When the Second World War broke out, the meetings were held in the Vicarage and at Porters tea-rooms on a fortnightly basis to mend clothing for the evacuee children. The usual meetings resumed the following year at the Infant School and demonstrations reflected the times with guest speakers discussing fruit bottling, the use of remnants, dress renovations and washable eiderdowns.

By the 1950s most meetings were held in the village hall although exceptionally at Cawne Close in 1954 and at Manor Farm in the winter of 1958. At this time demonstrations included paper flowers, painting on glass, beauty on a budget and home nursing. A number of events including coffee mornings, beetle drives, whist drives, jumble and harvest sales were organised in aid of local hospitals and charities.

Nationally, the Women's Institute celebrated their Golden Jubilee in 1965. To commemorate the event the Wilstead branch collated a scrapbook containing cuttings of various activities that had occurred in the village during the year. Derek Brooks, the village postmaster arranged to have the scrapbook bound in leather and Dick Brightman, a carpenter by trade, produced a wooden case to hold the book.

To mark the occasion, an oak tree was planted in front of the village hall on 6th March 1965 and Miss Howard, the County WI President performed the ceremony. Unfortunately the tree was damaged by reversing cars at a later date and was replanted in Ivy Lane but it did not survive. On behalf of the Wilstead branch,

WI Jubilee 1965 – Tree planting

(Reproduced with the kind permission of Janet Brooks)

Enid Wisson attended Golden Jubilee celebrations at the Queen's Garden Party at Buckingham Palace.

Some meetings in the 1970s were held in a members house in Town Close. Demonstrations were held on fabric painting and dyeing, paper sculpture, cake icing and deep relaxation.

The Wilstead branch celebrated its own golden jubilee in 1981 and a bench was donated as their gift to the village, placing it outside the Methodist church.

On 4th October 2001 the branch celebrated its 70th anniversary with over 70 members being entertained by local Bedfordshire band Patchwork who delighted them with music spanning the previous 70 years.

In February 1979 active village member Enid Wisson organised the first village Pancake Race. Participants ran down Church Road tossing pancakes, prizes were awarded and refreshments were served in the Chapter House next to the church. The event continued to take place every year thereafter for a period of approximately 10 years.

Children have always been well catered for. Our first recorded reference to a scout group in the village was in the 1930s. Lay reader, Douglas Wolveridge was scoutmaster and early meetings were held in the Infants school. The first scout hut was constructed in a cattle shed owned by the Mastin family and a lorry transported it onto a field which they donated. Claude Mastin then became leader of the troop.

In later years the scout hut was turned into a wooden bungalow and during the war it was converted to a small house. This was later pulled down and a new bungalow stands on the site which lies between the village hall, Whitworth Way and the recreation ground. Today there is an active cub scout group, 1st Haynes and Wilstead cub scout group which meets in the Methodist church hall.

Wilstead scouts camping at Parkfield Lowestoft Back row (l to r): Harry Bird; Walter Daniels; Claude Mastin (scout master) Mr Brewster; Mr F Stanbridge; Leslie Sugars; Harry Endy; Reginald Smith; Front row(l to r): Brian Crouch; Fred Caves; Jack Summerfield; Dereck Jones; Bill Smith

(Reproduced with the kind permission of Rose Summerfield)

Our earliest Girl Guide reference shows that in 1935 a New Year party for the Wilstead group was held at St Paul's Mission room. This was a joint party with the Girl Guides from Flitwick and included games, dancing and a campfire. The last village guide group ceased

Original Scout Hut

(Reproduced with the kind permission of Rose Summerfield)

around 1990 although there is an active brownie troop today.

The first sports club seems to be an informal tennis club, which met at a court behind Masters Garage and Dora Huckle's store. This area is now part of Dines Close and Towns Close.

In the 1970s, greater plans were on the horizon for sport. Roger Hopkins, the entertainment manager of the Jubilee playing field committee arranged with the contractors to build a pavilion. Sadly the attempts suffered vandalism as pipes and slates were damaged but despite this the pavilion was completed in time for the first playing fields fete in 1978.

After the pavilion was built, a meeting was held to establish interest in cricket. As enough interest was shown a cricket square was laid in Cumberland turf on the Silver Jubilee playing field at a cost of £2,500. The pitch was rolled by Roger Hopkins and Jim McCarthy, the task taking four nights. Despite the early interest, only one match was ever played on the pitch due to lack of support. As the cricket pitch was unused it eventually became part of a football field and is still used for that purpose today. The pavilion is currently used as changing rooms.

The village is extremely proud of its bowls club. A meeting was held on 16 April 1985 in the village hall with 62 people attending. It was agreed to form a private members club on the land by the allotments on a 99-year lease.

The founder members (as opposed to the early members) were elected on 22 April 1985 and were: Gordon Maskell president; Brian Couch chairman; George Anderson treasurer and Peter Scarborough vice chairman. Money was raised and the first clubhouse, a double portacabin was constructed in what is now the present car park. The first game was played in summer of 1987 and the bar was open. By the early 1990s members realised the need for a new clubhouse.

The first clubhouse

(Reproduced with kind permission of Bob and Jean Herbert)

New clubhouse at its opening

In addition to grants, a scheme was also devised whereby local people could pledge a brick of the portacabin clubhouse to raise the funds required. Construction work commenced in 1993 with Tom Wisson, chairman, Roger Hopkins as building manager and joint designer with Eric Forman whilst Bill Jones completed the electrical work to the club. A 'Dad's Army' of pensioners also helped with the club's construction. The grand opening was in Spring 1996 and the old clubhouse was sold and is now at the trout fisheries at Clophill.

Wilstead bowling green is a credit to the club's success. The green is recognised at county and national levels and is ranked to Middleton Cup standard. This qualifies it to host top ranking play. Recent events include Jean Tate, president of the England Women's Bowling Association hosting her game for England in May 2001 at the club with approximately 100 women from all the English counties attending. On 17 June 2001 the All England Women versus All England Men game was held on the green.

Short mat indoor bowling is played all year round for members. The clubs standard colours are pink and grey and the emblem on their badge depicts the story of the parish church and the three bells that were sold.

Wilshamstead's first football club was called Wilstead United who joined the Bedford & District League in 1928. The club played until 1939 and restarted at the end of the war when they joined the Bedford League in 1947 before withdrawing in 1956. There was a break in the history of the club playing games but by 1972 Wilstead Wanderers formed. They were so called because they had no pitch. With the advent of the silver jubilee playing field in 1977 the club became the present Wilshamstead Football Club. They have been successful in winning a number of championships and cups.

In 1984 a Youth Team was started by Robin Ryall and in 1990 the Youth section was set up with the U14s and U11s who have continued to play well in the League.

In 1994 two Sunday teams were developed, one of which is the Wilstead Hatters (named after the Black Hat Pub) who are adult players.

Nigel Jacobs, who was chairman for approximately 20 years says 'we have a club to be proud of. What makes me so pleased is that the vast majority of players of all the teams have close ties with the village and this is rare these days'.

The British Legion Hall was one of the earliest venues for entertainment. It was located where The Square is now. Access to the hall was via a footpath next to a house on Bedford Road. The hall stood across the back of the plot, situated on grounds belonging to the brewers who owned the Black Hat Public House.

The hall was a long wooden building, which resembled an army hut and was often referred to as the British Legion Hut. The hall had a round cast iron tortoise

British Legion hall

(Reproduced with the kind permission of Rose Summerfield)

stove, that was used to burn coke and this provided the only form of heating and minimum lighting was available. Despite this the hall was used for dances on Saturday nights as well as weddings and other social events including the ever-popular whist drives.

During the Second World War the hall was used by the Home Guard to provide entertainment for evacuee children from London and visiting London Fire Brigade families. Social evenings would be held reconstructing the songs from the First World War and on one particular occasion a concert in 1946 raised money for prisoners of war in Japan.

It was also the venue for Wilshamstead's first pantomime production of

Cast of Cinderella 1945
British Legion Hall

(Reproduced with the kind permission of Rose Summerfield)

Cinderella in December 1946, produced by Miss De Escobar. She was reputedly once a professional singer of the D'Oyley Carte Opera Company and Sadlers Wells Company and was staying in the village. She rented the Victorian vicarage and ran it as a guesthouse mainly for Londoners who came to the village for a rest at weekends. The vicarage was also used for the Wilstead youth club, which was established by her.

Miss De Escobar stayed in the village for approximately 3–5 years before moving to Bedford. She certainly planted the seed of inspiration for those that love the world of drama as the village has progressed to create their very own Wilstead Players amateur dramatic group.

The Wilstead Players were founded in October 1971 with approximately 20 members from the new families settling around Morgans Close and later Whitworth way. The first meeting was held in Bury Cottage in Northwood Lane and rehearsals were held in the function room of the Elephant and Castle Public House in Cotton End Road. The first performance was a Revue of sketches, songs

1971 Revue finale
Village Hall

(Reproduced with the kind permission of Jackie Tanswell)

and dances held in October 1971 and the first pantomime was The Pied Piper of Hamlin in February 1973.

Today, between three to five productions are held yearly and Wilstead Players have won numerous awards. The pinnacle of current success was when they performed at the All Winners Festival, which is a showcase for the best Amateur Theatre nationally, in Felixstowe in Summer 2000.

The Wilstead Young Players ranging from ages 8 to 16 meet weekly at the Saturday morning workshop and are trained by a professional drama teacher.

Many hours are spent in the village hall rehearsing to ensure all productions are perfect. One amusing incident when perfection went amiss was when one evening the cast was rehearsing the play The Waiting Room. A body was required in a coffin to create the real effect so they called for a volunteer. Jim McCarthy answered the call. Obeying his instructions he lay in the coffin whilst the other members were surrounding it. Suddenly Jim blew a kiss and what should have been a serious moment ended in laughter. As a result Jim was nicknamed Jim the Corpse.

Wilshamstead Village Hall in Cotton End Road has always been used to its full potential with a wide range of activities not only for the Wilstead Players but also for the local Pre-school Playgroup, the Women's Institute, and for senior citizens. The hall has been the venue for teaching of dance, youth activities, social evenings and wedding receptions.

The original Village Hall Fund was inaugurated with a balance of £102 6 shillings 6 pence. This had been raised by the holding of summer fetes, flag drives, beetle drives and a mile of pennies. By 1948 steps were taken to acquire a site for a village hall and by 1950 the Village Hall Committee had undertaken to hire the building at a nominal weekly rent.

In 1963 ownership of the building was acquired and in 1965 improvements and an extension estimated at £2207 were completed with the cost

Village Hall opening 1950

(Reproduced with the kind permission of Enid Wisson)

being met by a grant from the Ministry of Education and from local fund raising activities similar to those already mentioned.

During the late 1970s, village fetes were supported by our own unique team of Morris men. The original idea to form a team specifically for the Silver Jubilee Fete in 1977, came from Rosemary Boston who was at the time on the Playing Fields Committee. The great idea spread to a group of interested people in The Woolpack Public House where over a few beers the plan was adopted.

An early performance took place outside The Woolpack Public House in May 1977, in aid of a member of the football team who had broken his leg.

Dave Townes from Bedford Morris men was the musician and his brother Charlie Townes taught the steps. The first members were Roger Hopkins, Fool, Mick White, Squire, Bill Jones, Malcolm Bugge, Alan Bleeze, Rick Baxter, Mark Haines and Ken Adey. Derek Smith was also very involved at the beginning although he was not a performing member.

Rehearsals took place in the function room at the Elephant and Castle Public

*Wilshamstead Morris Men
May 1977*

*(Reproduced with the kind permission of
Roger Hopkins)*

House before moving to the Chapter House next to the Parish Church. Their traditional dances were of Cotswold style, mainly Adderbury and Bledington. The team enjoyed it so much that they continued for a further three years after the jubilee. Most of the performances were at summer fetes, parties, folk festivals, the annual Playing Fields Committee fete in July 1978 and at the annual Bovingdon airfield steam fayres.

The team's costume was designed in red, white and blue for the Silver Jubilee with bells worn on the shins below the knee. Their equipment included a horse on a stick to collect money from the audience and an authentic pig's bladder and sticks. In 1978 they took part in a world record event for the largest processional which involved a total of 309 Morris men at Sidmouth folk festival in Devon.

The last dance performed before they disbanded was at the Wilstead Festival in 1980 organised by the Playing Fields Committee and held on the Jubilee Playing Field. A marquee had been set up providing different forms of entertainment on each night including jazz, international folk, Irish & Hungarian dancing, Kayleigh, Scottish and last but not least Morris dancing. Sadly, when Dave Townes left a replacement musician couldn't be found and the team disbanded. Some of the members went to join the Redbornstoke Morris men in Ampthill.

For those with green fingers the yearly social event is the Wilstead Flower and Produce show. Held annually, the first show in current times was in 1978 to raise money for the village hall management committee. The five founder members were Rosemary Boston, Maurice Hickling, Colin Scargill, Peter Tanswell, and Basil Yoxen. Today, the show consists of various sections of flowers, vegetables, fruit, photography and cookery and in the past children's handwriting and illustrations. A special prize is awarded to the family resident in Wilstead gaining the most points in all of the competition sections. This is the Warren Cup, which is the sole surviving cup from produce shows held decades ago. It was resurrected from somebody's loft in the spirit of historic tradition.

Senior members of the village have also been very active. The Wilstead Darby and Joan Club was formed in October 1950 with Mrs Mabel Crawley as the original leader. This club lasted for approximately 40 years providing refreshments and bingo for senior parishioners on a Friday afternoon in the village hall. Christmas parties with entertainers and outings throughout the year were also arranged including the annual trip to the coast. The Wilstead branch sang to the tune of Farmers Boy:

> Come and join us in the village hall
> Each Friday afternoon
> We are such happy friendly folk
> As you will find out soon
>
> We sing, play games and often chat
> And drink such lovely tea
> Come and join the Wilstead D & J
> And happy you will be
> And happy you will be

CHAPTER 10

Traders Over Time

Over the centuries, Wilshamstead has had a variety of tradesmen and craftsmen. In the early eighteenth century the craft of lacemaking for women (overtaking spinning work and field work) was a flourishing industry and helped to supplement the family income which was primarily from agricultural work.

The youngsters respectfully called the elder lace making generation 'Grannies'. We learn of a 'Granny Taylor' from Ivy Lane who made lace and was renowned for

Betsey Day making pillow lace outside Church Cottage

(Reproduced with the kind permission of Miriam Langford)

always having pins in her mouth! She would throw coal in the fire and as a result her dirty fingers would stain the lace. Consequently, the lace was washed before it was sent to the retailers for sale. Several ladies continued with the craft for many years. There was also a pocket of straw plaiters and some women undertook basket weaving on Duck End Farm. The farm had an osier bed above the gravel seam and this provided the necessary withies (long shoots) for the basket weaving. Its site now accommodates an aircraft hanger.

Following the Napoleonic Wars, the local industries were in depression by 1829. Due to widespread poverty many people were in search of additional occupations in order to provide the extra income they required. The Sale of Beer Act of 1830 made it possible to set up beer houses in order to provide additional monies. It was not uncommon to have more than one job and a significant amount of the male population was involved in farming, working with steam engines, thrashing and stacking and helping their wives run a beer house in the evening. Others had smallholdings and also worked at the local brickworks.

With more than one occupation it would not be surprising to hear of a tale when a local person experienced a spate of forgetfulness! On one occasion, Alfie Hebbes who had a smallholding and managed the White Horse Public House in Bedford Road called at Church Farm and said "I can't find my cows anywhere!" The farmer replied "I don't know what you've done with them". A week later the farmer was curious to find out what had happened to his cows and he enquired if they had been found. Alfie Hebbes replied "ooooh yea mate, I'd left them in the cow shed!"

By 1851 the majority of people in Wilshamstead were farmers and cattle dealers and the village had a Post Office, beer retailers, baker, innkeeper, wheelwright, butcher, grocer & draper, carpenters and a blacksmith. In the village was also John Kendall, an umbrella mender and Amelia Toll (nee Pearce) a bonnet sewer.

Other tradesmen established in the village by 1885 included brick and tile maker, carriers, carter, corn dealer, dairymen and boot & shoemaker. The village also had two tailors, Joseph Cousins and John Smith, and Charles Toll was a machinist.

The number of craftsmen was also increasing during this period. Thomas Fountain, who was born in Wilstead, went onto become a watch and clock maker in Sharnbrook in 1861.

By the 20th century the straw plaiting and lace making industries had declined and the number of craftsmen had decreased by 1940. Shopkeepers too had decreased but the number of services had increased. For example, in 1936 there was Albert Joseph Cox, a house decorator and Frank Masters, a coal dealer. The number of farmers and smallholders in comparison to the previous century had remained the same.

One of the local craftsmen in the village was Peter Mackinnon, a church architectural restorer. He restored the roof at the parish church of All Saints in the 1960s and also produced creative work for Terence Rattigan, the playwright.

In the early days, the horse and cart was the main means of travel and the smithy was an essential trade for our village. The blacksmith was often seen busily shoeing horses and sparks would be flying as he worked at the anvil.

The earliest records of a forge in Wilshamstead appears in 1640 when a, 'smith's forge and a little barn of 2 bays' was sold for £24.

In 1851 the village blacksmiths on the corner of Church Road was owned by the Haynes Park estate and was

Blacksmith premises on corner of Church Road with 'top school' in the background

(*Reproduced with the kind permission of Dorothy Houghton*)

run by a succession of members of the Tuffnell family. Edward Tuffnell, born in Wilstead also followed in the family trade and became estate blacksmith for Melchbourne Park.

In the Haynes Park estate sale in 1914, the blacksmiths shop was purchased by James Mastin and Sons and in later years it was run by George Mastin. When he retired Howard and Wesley Sharpe who were connected to the Mastin family took over the business until they retired in 1951. Other blacksmiths in the parish such as Mr Irons from Cotton End Road and Francis Cole from Luton Road operated on a smaller scale.

As the need for horses declined, the business on Church Road corner developed into a farm and agricultural engineering concern. The site was later purchased for industrial development and the smithy was demolished.

The carrier's cart transported goods and folk to a set destination in Bedford. Amongst the early carriers was George Rogers, Joseph Masters in 1885 making regular trips by horse and cart with hens, eggs and pigs to the market and Joseph Finding from Ivy Lane in 1891.

Harry Crowsley outside The Woolpack
(Reproduced with kind permission of Dorothy Houghton)

The Crowsley family who ran the Woolpack Public House were also carriers from Wilshamstead to Bedford. Using a wagonette that carried up to six people and the driver, goods could also be placed on board. For many years it carried washing from Bedford to the ladies in the village who did the laundry before it was returned to the terminal at the King's Arms in St Mary's in Bedford. Mrs Frances Masters took over the carrier route from Charles Crowlsey senior but it returned to Charles's son, Harry Crowsley after a time.

In the early 20th century, Eric Crouch travelled by horse and cart to Bedford to sell milk as he had one of several dairy farms in the village at the time. David Lodge made trips to Bedford with an old Ford vehicle that was a flat bed truck during the day but at weekends a canvas hood was placed over it to take people for the main Saturday trip into town. He also collected milk churns from the village farms to take to Bedford. As his wife was the schoolmistress of the National school in the 1920s he regularly took school children to Bedford Corn Exchange for concerts.

Involvement with grain was apparent as in 1839 records show Thomas and Jason Quenby as corn merchants and in 1911 James and Frederick Quenby were small holders and corn merchants. Other local corn merchants have been Jonathan Hallworth, Frederick Joseph Northwood and George Hallworth..

At a later date, in the house opposite Church House was Mr Stonebridge, known as 'Dodder'. He had a workshop in his yard where his engine crushed corn and rolled oats for the local farmers. Mr Stonebridge also helped out on the farms and was the village 'handyman' for any odd jobs in carpentry.

As well as the corn industry, Wilstead had a thriving bakery. The original bake house was adjacent to the Elephant and Castle Public House in Cotton End Road and the baker in 1807 was Richard Quenby. By 1851, Frederick Cox is shown as the village baker with the bake house being rented from Richard Quenby. After purchasing a cottage and land in Church Road from Lord John Thynne in 1861, Frederick Cox mortgaged the property to raise funds to build a new bake house on adjacent land. In 1885 both bakeries were operating as both Frederick Cox and Thomas Quenby are recorded as bakers. These two properties are still in the village today.

Baking was later undertaken by three generations of the Richardson family who began in 1891. They took over the business in Church Road but then moved back to the Cotton End Road site. This property was sold on 3rd September 1894 for £127 before the bakery once more returned to Church Road.

A coal fired oven was used in the Church Road bakery and had the capacity to take up to 200 loaves. This old oven was replaced in the late 1960s with an electric oven. It took up to 14 men to remove the old oven over a 3-day period. Each brick had to be hammered out and large boulders weighing up to 14 lbs each were found in the process. Some were still hot as they were removed.

Bake House Church Road 2001

Thomas Richardson was the village baker. Later Thomas's son Edgar took over and then his son Ken and the Richardson family made house to house deliveries of fresh cottage loaves and buns by horse and cart up to the 1950s. These were the days when the back door was left open and the bread was placed on the kitchen table. Due to a change in lifestyle with more families out at work and rapid changes in the business, the house to house deliveries came to an end in the 1960s. The Richardson family tradition of making the wheatsheaves for the parish church at harvest festivals continued for many years but the largest was a harvest festival loaf in 1946 measuring 29 inches in height.

When the Richardson family retired in 1986, the Cox family took it over and continued as a bakery for a short while before the business ceased to trade.

Another of Wilstead's trades that no longer exists in the village today was that of the cobbler.

Bake House Cotton End Road 2002

*Remains of Frederick Baker's
Cobbler shop 2001*

Two cobblers in 1885 were Levi Potter, boot and shoemaker from Potter's End and James Sugars. In 1936 a cobbler shop was set up by Frederick Baker of Haynes on Rudd Green's farmland at Cotton End Farm. It was later taken over by his son Jim Baker who ceased to trade in the late 1960s. Mr Herbert, a Londoner then set it up as a general store but due to break-ins it never actually opened. The remains of the shop can still be seen.

There were numerous carpenters in the village and this is reflected in the name of a public house which existed on Cotton End Road, the Carpenters Arms Public House. Sometimes, the trades ran in families and James Toll, George Toll, William Toll and John Toll were all carpenters. As was Sam Toll, who was also a beer retailer.

By mid 1930s, the main carpenter and undertaker was George Geary. He made coffins in his workshop opposite the Black Hat Public House and on the day of a funeral he would request the local men to help him carry the deceased in the wooden hearse to the parish church via Church Road.

Although many villagers were self sufficient, growing their own vegetables and fruit and keeping hens, chickens and rabbits in the backyard, the local stores played a significant part in village daily life.

There are instances of farmers also being butchers in the village such as Cooper Perkins in 1811 and Alfred Rose and Arthur J Cox in 1891.

Freddie Smith's slaughterhouse in Ivy Lane was in existence since at least 1908.

Tom Wisson outside his shop 1985

(Reproduced with the kind permission of Janet Brooks)

They kept cows in the sheds at the rear and slaughtered pigs and sheep. This business later passed onto his nephew Cyril Taylor whose descendants still live in the village.

Adjacent to The Nags Head Public House in Cotton End Road was Isaac Brightman and Alfred Cox as butchers in 1885. Arthur Frederick Stanley Cox (brother of Alfred Cox) followed in the trade. By 1936 Herbert R Ives took over the business until trade ceased in the 1960s, when most of the buildings in this area were demolished.

In more recent years in the 1970s a butcher shop was opened and run by Tom Wisson in Cotton End Road next to the Evangelical Church. The shop ceased to trade in the 1990s and has since been converted into a private residential property. Before it was Tom Wisson's butchers, the property was used by the Fiorelle, Taylor and Bean families as a general stores and later a sweet shop.

The village has had a number of grocers and general stores over the years. Early traders included grocer and tea dealer George Morgan in 1827, Thomas Phipps, grocer and draper in 1851 and George Arnold, Walter Phipps and George Tomkins, all grocers around 1885. In 1891, Frederick J Cooker was recorded as a grocer.

Phipps grocers shop was later owned by Mr H A Lees before Ernest Miller took it over around 1936 and the property became commonly known as Miller's shop. Mr Miller sold groceries, paraffin and almost everything one needed until the Upton family took it over in the 1950s followed by Mr Carter in the 1960s who turned it into a haberdashery store. By the late 1960s it became a hair-dressers and then an electrical goods shop before being converted to a private residential property. This is pictured in the Name Game chapter under the heading Phipps Close.

A popular shop was Dora's Stores situated where number 1 Dines Close is today. The tiny store was run by Mrs Gillson during the Second World War exchanging clothing vouchers and selling wool, buttons and silk. After the war Dora Huckle took it over and sold fresh produce, haberdashery and Craven A cigarettes not forgetting the ice-cream for Sunday afternoon tea. A dry-cleaning service and small village library was also provided. Dora's store was demolished when Dines Close was built.

Dora's Stores with Dora on the threshold

In Luton Road, opposite the Red Lion Public House was Frederick Robinson, a gentle quietly spoken man trading as F Robinson & Son. He sold groceries and delivered groceries in the village on a Wednesday afternoon when it was half day closing. In the 1930's it was known as Peartree because of the pear tree growing on the sidewall of the building. On numerous occasions the young lads would try and grab one of the delicious pears described as 'absolute crackers' as they exited the store. In 1957 for a period of approximately 4 years it became Margaret's Greengrocers & Fruiterers before it was transformed into a private dwelling.

In the early part of the 20th century local tradesmen travelled the village selling

Robinsons Grocers now a private property, 2002

Robinson's Grocers then

*(Reproduced with the kind permission of
Sandra Whitaker)*

goods via horse and cart. William Burr, for example, was a fishmonger, selling fresh produce and wet fish on a Friday, using his hand pushed cart. In contrast, over 60 years later was A S Fensome Ltd (trading from 1954) sold groceries from a van. Mr Steve Fensome, who still lived in the village at the time of writing, said his products were sold at 'Bedford price with a vast difference', sugar at 2p lb, butter at 10p lb and 8p for a box of biscuits.

Other travelling salesmen were Benny or Ben Spick who bought hens in the village and sold them in Bedford. He was well known for saying 'I'll give e're 18 pence, shan't give ya no more'. Mr Williamson called weekly and collected wild mushrooms from Cotton End Farm to sell in Bedford, Mr Pepperdine sold cakes, buns and ice cream on a Saturday and Mr Zachtilla the ice-cream man also called regularly.

William Ambrose Coley, a local poultry farmer sold animal feed for hens and rabbits and paraffin up to 3 times a week in the 1930s. Mr Hays during his retirement collected wood in his barrow boy London type cart and chopped it up behind the Rose Public House, before selling it as firewood in the village. A gentleman by the name of Jack called on a Thursday to sell needles, cotton and knicker elastic and soon acquired the name of Thursday Jack.

Wilshamstead has had a number of garages in the past. George Masters owned

*Masters garage at
Wilshamstead Crossroads
late 1950s/60s*

*(Reproduced with the kind per-
mission of Dorothy Houghton)*

the Central Garage, at the crossroads. It was
an old wooden building with 2 large doors and
a canopy. Surrounding outbuildings contained
cars and motorbike accessories. It had hand-
operated petrol pumps, and the cost of petrol
in the 1950s was only 11 p a gallon! It charged
up accumulator batteries and sold radios.
Many young boys as early as age 14 paid one
shilling per week on account at Masters
garage until they had saved sufficient monies
to purchase their first bicycle. Part of the
garage was set up as a newsagent and run by
one of the Masters family. The same site is
trading as a car sales garage today.

Along Luton Road was Porters garage
owned by Jack Porter and sometimes known
as Gandi by the locals. Besides selling petrol
there was use of a limited library and the
Porters Tea Rooms. These were frequently
used for wedding receptions and for Mothers
Union meetings. The garage later became a
NAFTA garage but after it caught fire the site
was used for housing development.

*Ralph and Dorothy Cooper on their
wedding day outside Porters Tea
Rooms*

(Reproduced with the kind permission of
Dorothy Cooper)

On part of Bedford Road known now as the loop was the Shell Montrose garage
which opened in the 1920s. At the time, it had a workshop and filling station but
later a transport Café was added to it in the 1950s. When the bypass was built
Shell relocated the filling station to the site now occupied by Seasons Garden
Centre. The original garage became an aerial manufacturers shop and is now
Davies Garage where M.O.T.s are undertaken.

As well as farming, the Maskell family of Duck End Farm was one of the first to
take on M.O.T vehicle testing in the village in the 1960s. Gordon Maskell established an engineering business which remains one of only three workshops in the

*Michael Maskell's engine at
Rook Tree Farm
(Summerfields) Haynes 2001*

county approved to pressure test steam engine boilers. Michael Maskell's own traction engine is well known locally.

Wilshamstead has also had an antiques trade. By 1936 the Old Curiosity shop run by Ernest Masters situated where Bird Court is today was selling old rifles from the Boer war, garden tools, lamp glasses, oil and candles. It was like a small shed, with no supply of electricity or water.

Douglas Wolveridge, the lay preacher at St Paul's church in the 1930s had a love for antiques, particularly silver, and often bought and sold antiques. He stored his collections, books and curios in the old coach house at the vicarage before he moved to the Old Manor house. This tradition is carried on today in the same property with Manor Antiques and Interiors although the building has been a hotel in the past.

The building trade has been well represented. Gambriel & Sugars based in Dane Lane built many houses in Putnoe, Bedford, the Wilshamstead village hall, houses in The Square, Cotton End Road, and in Northwood Lane. Close Crete was a concrete business where Town Close is today.

The first record of a doctor attending to the village was the appointment of Joseph Pulley on Easter Tuesday 1789. Dr Pulley of Bedford agreed to be surgeon and apothecary for four guineas until the following Easter. For a further guinea he agreed to attend 'in cases of dangerous midwifery' and also 'to find medicines in the natural smallpox and inoculate those receiving collection from the parish'.

Doctors later held weekly surgeries in various dwellings including the Victorian house called Ferndale on Cotton End Road. Doctors Macklin and Van Landenberg attended to the village by 1930s and Miss Honora Meehan was the district nurse.

Dr McCaskie's car and Richardson's bakers van along Cotton End Road

(Reproduced with kind permission of Margaret Pearce)

The care of hair has fallen to a number of barbers including Josh Tuffnell who cut hair for 4d in the evenings and worked for the council during the day and Charlie Warren, who charged sixpence a hair cut but who also prepared wedding bouquets.

There are several trades and services in existence in the village today that continue to be an asset to the local community including Davies Bros garage on Bedford Road (loop) and Burr's garage in Ivy Lane. Many modern village services are advertised in the parish newsletter offering everything from the village plumber to odd jobs to aromatherapy and picture framing.

Currently in the shops at the crossroads is the Chinese Takeaway (The Golden

Sun), formerly a fish and chip shop trading as Crossways Takeaway in the 1970s and then as a Café; Wilstead Tandoori which was formerly a ladies hairdressing salon until the 1990s and Kaileys mini market. On the opposite corner where the blacksmith was once sited is the milk dairy depot and Dingle Dell Computing.

The Wilshamstead postal service began when George Rogers was appointed as the first postman in the village in 1845. The charge for delivery was 'id for each letter, unless more than 1, then charge 2 for 1d'. The appointed postman had to call at Mr Phipps shop at 9 o'clock each morning, (except Saturdays) to receive the letter bag.

The very first Post Office was situated in a cottage on the corner of Haynes Park carriageway drive and Cotton End Road next to the gatekeeper's cottage. Mrs Coley ran it for 40 years before her grandson George Sharpe took over with his wife Sarah in 1885, having previously been sub postmaster. Around 1890, George Sharpe had the present Post Office built using bricks from the local Wilshamstead brickyard. In the early days Mr Sharpe had to cycle into Bedford to collect the mail at 6 o'clock in the morning but in later years deliveries were made direct from the Bedford Post Office. He retired at the age of 73 after 45 years. His sons went onto other things in the village. In the late 1930s, the Post Office was run by Fred Robinson. In the 1950s, under the ownership of Mrs Doris Croot the Post Office saw many structural alterations and she is long remembered for her lengthy service and involvement in the village.

Rose Summerfield who worked with Mrs Croot for many years in the Post Office, appeared in the national newsagents periodical and won a prize for demonstrating her helpful and polite manner to customers.

Derek and Janet Brooks succeeded Mrs Croot in 1978 and were postmasters for almost 19 years before Alice and David Dougall kept the business until the current postmaster arrived in 2002.

The following poem was written about the village in the 1990s:

My Village

My Village is just a village about 4 miles south of town
The main road is quite long and runs straight up and down
The smell of newly baked bread lingers in the air
Fresh meat fills the butcher's shop, there is always plenty there
The Post Office is handy, there's a hairdresser for that shampoo and set
And of course theres the chip shop that I can't forget
It seems that theres a pub wherever you happen to be
There's even a camping and caravan site, 'Wilstead by the Sea'
The church doors are open for that quiet prayer
And for those wishing to walk with nature, the woods and fields are near
Shrill voices of children in the school playground echo on the breeze
Little girls chanting their skipping rhymes, little boys with grazed knees
It is not what you would call an attractive village, though pretty lanes here and there weave
It's the sort of place that grows on you and is very hard to leave.

My village is just a village about 4 miles south of town
But before I end my poem I thought I'd write this down
It does have one very special feature which is hard to find today
A really caring community to help you along life's way.

Vivien Hawkey

Following a competition, the following picture was selected for inclusion in this book and shows the post office in 2002.

Drawn by David Daniels aged 8 2002

CHAPTER 11

Wood, Wind and Water

Wood wind and water have long played a part in the daily life of the village and overlooking it from the slopes of the Greensand Ridge is Wilstead Wood.

It is a remnant of ancient woodland and was also once known as Great Wood. Now in private ownership it is jointly managed with the Forestry Commission. It has in the past been noted as a wildlife site and contains one of the village's few remaining natural ponds.

In 1914, Haynes Park Estate, of which Wilstead Wood formed a part, was divided into 203 lots and sold at auction. The three day sale attracted a lot of attention and amongst the lots sold was timber in Wilstead Wood. The timber being described as 'full of marketable oak of the most desirable character'.

The carriage drive at the rear of the estate passed from Cotton End Road in Wilshamstead through the centre of the wood on its way to the main estate buildings. This drive was a back route for the estate but also allowed access to the wood. Following the sale of the timber lots a second route out of the wood was required for the timber carriages.

Today, one of the village's most popular footpaths still runs along this second route which runs from Luton Road up to the meadows below the wood. When it was in use by the timber carriages, the fields

Timber carriage by Cardington hangers

(Reproduced with the kind permission of Dorothy Cooper)

on both sides contained livestock and wire fences were put up on either side of the route to stop the animals straying into the path of the carriages. The woody growth that is present along this footpath was created by blackbirds sitting on the fence and passing seeds. So numerous were these birds that the long meadow field that runs adjacent to the Briar Bank Mobile Home Park has the name Blackbirds. This field is an enclosure that dates to medieval times and at the time of the village enclosure act it was called Far Wood Close.

Wilstead Wood is responsible for the shape of the field system to the south of the village. The smaller shaped fields that exist between the village line and the woods owe their existence to medieval assarting. This system of clearing areas of woodland by hand takes a lot of time and effort to enable the land to be farmed. Only a little at a time would be cleared and these areas would be enclosed with a hedge. Many of the hedgerows in this part of the parish can still be dated to the medieval clearances.

An event that made many national newspaper headlines and reached the attention of the Queen occurred in Wilstead Wood in 1919.

The strange murder of Nellie Florence Ruby Rault remains a mystery today as the man who was accused of the crime was acquitted. An intricate case with many twists and turns can not be fully reproduced here but we hope we have provided an outline sufficient to mark the passing of the sad incident.

Following the sale in 1914, the Haynes Park house and estate was occupied by the Royal Engineers during the first world war and for a short time afterwards.

21 year old Nellie Rault was a member of Queen Mary's Army Auxiliary Corps and was described as 5ft in height, dark and extremely attractive. A native of Jersey, she was employed at the Haynes Park Camp as an assistant in the officers cookhouse from April 1917 and was found to be lovely with a sunny disposition.

The carriageway drive, closed to civilians, was a regular route from the camp to Wilshamstead and Bedford. On May 9th 1919, Nellie Rault left the camp in the afternoon after telling her friend she was going to meet Sergeant Major Hepburn in Bedford.

By the morning of Saturday 10th May, she was missed and it was reported to the local police. A search was eventually organised and by 5pm her body was found in undergrowth having sustained a number of injuries. One of the key issues is the number and variety of timings of events. An example of this is how long it took a directed search party of 100 people to find her body despite its proximity to the camp.

The body was discovered less than 15 yards from the edge of the carriageway drive and near to the gate at the top where no hedge or railings separated the woods from the drive.

PC Holben's statement described the fully clothed body as lying on its back with knees bent underneath, the right hand was stretched out with an army dinner knife nearby. Her hat was on the right hand side, her left hand was on her breast and her wallet lying on her chest and chin, money remaining in it. The body was covered in branches and had stab wounds in the chest, shoulder and back with bruises on her face.

The authors have been advised that should such a body be found today, it would be considered a murder of ritualistic nature, so unusual was its form. At the time it was surmised that she had been showing the photo in her wallet to her attacker. This does not seem to account for her kneeling position though.

A number of circumstances in the period of time before the murder were detailed and this led to the apprehension and charging of Company Sergeant Major Montague Cecil Keith Hepburn. Described as a good looking 30 year old, broad shouldered and with a small brown curly moustache, he came from Chelsea in London and had seen active service throughout the war.

Queen Mary was greatly distressed to hear of the murder and sent a letter of sympathy to the girls' distressed mother in Jersey.

The Coroners Inquest was held at The Haynes Park Signal Depot and lasted 5 days. Many details were read out and statements given but upon its conclusion an open verdict was returned on 21 May 1919 of 'Murder by certain person unknown to the jurors'. Incidentally, a police report states that one day, Juryman Cox was unable to attend as he had met with an accident and was in bed. It is likely that this individual was from Wilshamstead.

As he had been formally charged with murder, Company Sergeant Major Hepburn was remanded in custody and a few days later was brought before the court system at Bedford Divisional Court. The court was full with many women present in the room. The expectation was for a recital and piercing together of the evidence but when Mr F G Sims, the assistant director of Public Prosecutions rose to his feet, it became obvious that an announcement was to be made. The Bedford Record reported that 'the proverbial pin could have been heard to drop'.

Mr Sims stated: "The director of Public Prosecutions has carefully considered the evidence thus far obtained in the case and has arrived at the conclusion that the best interest of justice would not be served by immediately proceeding further with this inquiry. This course, should it be sanctioned by the Bench, must be followed by the discharge of the prisoner". After further comments, he concluded with "....the opinion of Director of Public Prosecutions.....it would not be in the best interests of justice if he [DPP] were not called upon to offer any evidence that day and left the matter open for further investigation".

Mr Sims went on to direct that the police would spare no effort to discover the perpetrator and that it was hoped that the person would be brought to justice. Despite this statement, police records of the case, still retained until today, show that no further action was ever taken and although the case is not open, it remains unresolved.

Nellie Raults grave at Haynes churchyard 2001

Stories about the murder case either experienced first hand or passed down by parents are still around in the village and these give a variety of reasons of why local people think 'he got off' but all the stories have a root in the class system of the era.

Nellie Rault was buried with full honours in the small churchyard at Haynes. Her grave is marked by a memorial cross erected by her fellow workers in Q.M.A.A.C and the officers and men of the Royal Engineers Signal Depot.

Another sad death was that of 12 year old Sydney Fuller who on January 26th 1900 was involved in a fatal accident. Whilst he was employed with a heavily laden timber carriage, he by some means became entangled in a wheel which threw him to the ground and passed over his head. His death was instantaneous. Although the family were newly resident in Wilstead, the parish magazine recorded that 'much sympathy was felt for his family'.

The main sawmill in the village was located on a plot that still stands empty today. Footpath number 6 runs along one side of it and if you are travelling down Cotton End Road towards the crossroads it is on your left shortly before you reach Chapel Lane on your right.

Upon this site stood a building that contained a workshop and stables with offices overhead. Older residents can recall this building in a dilapidated state after many years as a pig sty in the middle of the 20th century. One local name for the plot was the Piggery which was used by children in the 1950's.

During the first world war the timber yard made coffin sections and these were shipped to France.

Timber was sawn in this period by the use of a steam engine. On 23 February 1917 William Henry Izzard who owned the sawmill was killed whilst cutting lengths of wood. Mrs Florence Toll who lived opposite the sawmill reported at the inquest, which was held at the Elephant and Castle Public House, that she had heard an unusual noise with the engine. John Izzard, William's brother, who was also working at the sawmill at the time, saw the driving belt come off the shafing pulley and became wound up on the flywheel of the tractor. It caught William Izzard and lifted him full out of the tender, smashing his head against the travelling wheel and killing him instantaneously. John was hurt in the attempt to save his brother and it was Mrs Toll who shouted for help.

Also on the slope of the Greensand Ridge to the east of Wilstead Wood is a much smaller wood called St Macute's Wood known locally as Snake's Wood because of the adders that could once be seen sunning themselves there. It has also held the name Little Wood.

St Macute was a disciple of St Brendan the voyager and St Macute's day is celebrated on November 15th. A free chapel of St Macute's was granted to Beaulieu Priory (a cell of St Albans Abbey) and is thought to have been located in the adjacent parish of Eastcotts. In 1279 Amaury de St Amand, a descendant of the D'Albini family gave a carucate of land in Wilshamstead to the Priory. A carucate is another term for a hide of land; the amount that a team of eight oxen can plough in a year and deemed sufficient to support a typical peasant family. The D'Albini family had extensive lands including one of the manors of Wilshamstead. The land given to the Priory was to provide sufficient support to enable a monk in the chapel, to celebrate a mass 3 days a week for de St Amand's soul and the souls of his ancestors. By the time an inquisition was held into its ownership around 1427, a monk was unable to fulfil this duty because the value of the land at Wilshamstead had depreciated in value to £4 a year and was providing insufficient support. The site was still being used in the 15th century with barns being built by the Abbott in 1438 but at the time of the dissolution of the monasteries by Henry VIII, the lands passed to the crown.

In 1706 a map records the name of St Macute's Pasture and in the enclosure award the field names of Monks Field, Monks Close and Monks Further Close are given marking part of the original carucate. The site of the chapel is still disputed but an originally larger St Macute's Wood is also likely to have been part of the carucate of land. Today only the name remains to remind us of its origins in the Middle Ages. In the 1914 Haynes Park sale St Macute's timber was sold for £1,075.

Timber was also sold in other areas. In the 17th century, the account books of the estate of Wrest Park at Silsoe record how 77 trees were brought from Wilshamstead and Warden for a new garden that was being created to the south of the house. It is likely that a number of these would have been taken from the woods in our parish.

In the village itself, trees have also played their part.

Bedfordshire contained a few follies, one of which existed at Wilshamstead. The term 'folly' is generally now taken to refer to sham ruins in the gardens of large houses but it originally was also applied to small odd shaped pieces of land.

Wilshamstead's folly was triangular in shape and wooded, it was used by the wheelwrights in the building opposite to lay timber out to season. The popular footpath that had been the second carriageway runs along its edge. The triangular shape can still be clearly detected in aerial photographs and is now occupied by the houses and gardens of numbers 9, 11 and 13 Luton Road.

Trees also impact on the landscape around us. During the first world war the Bedfordshire Times reported in 1917 that 'a great difference in the appearance of the village has been made by the felling of several fine trees near the crossroads'. It is understood they were for use in France. Later when the A6 was altered in the mid twentieth century, at Wilshamstead Hill, it was reported that a single black Poplar tree was retained. The tree of 'enormous proportions filled the sky over the Vale of Bedford' in a time when trees were often cut down for road alterations.

Wilshamstead's shady churchyard is well timbered with a number of yew trees. King Henry V (1413–1422) passed an Act of Parliament ordering the planting of Yew trees in churchyards. The wood was required for the manufacturing of bows for archery and as the Yew is poisonous to cattle, the churchyard was the only place where they could be grown away from animals. The tradition has been continued.

Ponds are naturally forming in the village due to the geological structure. The Village design statement produced in September 2000 lists the 4 remaining main ponds as (1)off Luton Road (now within the Oakley Grange complex) and (2)at the junction of Bedford Road and the A6. Both of these areas contain protected Great Crested Newts. (3)A pond to the west of Dane Lane. This was one of the original extraction sites for Wilstead's brick industry and (4) as mentioned in Wilstead Wood.

In 1844, ponds were close to the main road and surveyors at the time reported that 'two of them were not only dangerous but also a great nuisance'. Although the location of these was not mentioned, we do know that within living memory, a pond was adjacent to Cotton End Road to the right of the infants school. It was surrounded by Elm trees and a number of residents recall playing in it as children when they used to attend the nearby school.

Cotton End Manor Farmhouse pond 2002

Many of the naturally occurring ponds are now gone but three ponds located on Cotton End Manor are listed as dating back to the medieval period. One of these is near the farmhouse itself.

Whilst animals could freely drink at any water source, the people of the village used wells. The main Town Well was located at the crossroads and water was often carried in pails and on yokes. A blizzard in 1916 caused the handle on the well to be broken when tree boughs fell across it.

Following floods at the turn of the year 1917/1918, the Town Well filled with turbid surface water. As it was such an important source, ten residents who lived nearby volunteered to empty it and working in relays they drew up hundreds of buckets of water. Once the well was clear, a bank of mud was raised around it to prevent a further repetition. In 1943 it was reported that railway sleepers were procured free of charge and laid at the Town Well and secured with roping. The Parish council made note that Mastin Brothers, who owned and occupied the Smithy site, helped to carry out the work and made no charge to the parish.

People still remember the daily task of collecting water from the well with galvanised iron buckets. Each bucket would hold a couple of gallons of water and some families had a wooden yoke that would connect to the bucket and enable them to carry two at a time. They can recall it was a struggle to avoid getting water in their shoes as children and it certainly caused a commotion if the bucket was lost in the well.

The daily task got easier when water pumps were situated around the village. The last of Wilstead's water pumps is now situated in the burial ground. Although no longer working it serves to remind us of the days past.

At the other end of the village, the cottages at the hamlet of Littleworth could use a well on the corner of the bend near to the site of St Paul's Church . The cottages at Potter's End had the use of a well situated in the nearby farmyard. The farm is now known as Cotton End Farm.

Last village pump

Open ditch at Elms Lane looking towards Potters End 2002

From the number of ponds and artesian wells we can see that the topography of Wilshamstead has meant that drainage has always been a necessity. Open ditches were the first method of draining water away but they were not always fenced off.

One of the earliest records for the village shows that open ditches were part of life in the Middle Ages. Cicely, was the two and a half year old daughter of William the carpenter of Wilshamstead in 1270. About tierce (a reference to the Christian service performed about 9am) on 29 May she went out of the door carrying a piece of bread. Whilst toddling alongside a deep ditch near to the house, a small pig came and tried to take the bread from her hand.

Cicely fell into the ditch and drowned. She was found by her mother Emma who found two pledges (people who were willing to act as surety for her) in Thomas Wymarc and Henry Swon. An inquest was held and it found that Cicely died by misadventure. The pig was separately appraised with a value of 2d and delivered to Wilshamstead.

In order for the water to run freely in the ditches, it was important that they were kept from becoming overgrown. In 1679, two county justices of the peace, William Bothey and Mr T Hillersdon testified and set their seals on 16 March to certify 'that the brooke leading from Kingston Hardwicke to Pipers Bridge is very well cleansed and scoured and amended by some of the inhabitants of Wilshamsteed soe that the water may have its free course there'. Pipers Bridge is located where Bedford Road crosses the water course near to Duck End Lane.

The next step in draining following on from open ditches was deep draining. The earliest method of which was bush draining. This involved lining the bottom with bushes which were then covered with earth. The bushes which were clumps of sticks or wood, were sufficient to keep open a channel through which the water could drain away. One of the first records of the use of bush drains in the county was in Wilshamstead. In 1763 James Odell was paid for 'blackthorn bushes to lay in the Drayen in the Church yard'. These can not have been too effective though as the water level in the church yard rose so high that the churchwardens had to buy iron ladles. These were used to bale out the graves so that the coffins could be lowered into them. Today, a ditch still runs alongside the western boundary of the church-yard and at the time of the Victorian vicarage, a pond formed part of the property.

In 1914, William Soper arrived in the village. Invited by the Boston family at Church Farm to help with drainage he brought two steam powered Fowler engines, ploughs, cultivators, a mole drainer and two living vans.

In an article written by Mr Boston of Church Farm it was reported that William Soper's first job was to help a local engine out of a ditch in Elms Lane where a culvert had collapsed. Mr Soper stayed in the village for seven years during which time he drained much of the land using locally made clay tiles and also mole drains. A mole drain creates a channel in the sub soil that allows water to drain from the top soil holding the crop and then slowly seep away.

Wilshamtead no longer possess a windmill but it once formed a major part in the farming life of the village. The farmers would bring the grain to be ground into flour.

The earliest written reference to a mill in the parish is in 1648 but it is likely one stood in the village before this time. Henry James the miller died in 1648 leaving the mill to his grandson Henry Dearmer. On 7 May 1678, Henry's son George was presented at court on a charge of house breaking. The local gentry, Mr William Beech, prosecuted George for breaking and entering into the house of Mr William Wells and stealing a silver instrument called a correll. It is thought that this instrument is likely to have been a quarrel from a crossbow. Mr Beech had been called by the watchman to arrest the burglars but upon arrival only found the neighbours at the house. The burglars had escaped leaving behind them two horses and two coats. In his defence George Dearmer declared he had been born at Wilshamstead and his father was the miller. He had gone to London to fetch payment for goods his father had supplied but had returned unpaid. He declared he had returned via Woburn. In the Church is a stone memorial tablet to William Wells.

The Ogilby route map of 1675 shows the mill on the east side of the main road to Bedford near to the parish boundary with Elstow.

In 1686 Henry Dearmer sold the mill to Robert Potton, who upon his death in 1699 bequeathed it to Sarah wife of Michael Bonfield. It remained in this family for 64 years until Thomas Bonfield sold it to Thomas Hornbuckle. By this time the windmill was apparently in ruins. The conveyance document states 'all that of windmill and materials thereof lately standing and situate in Millfield' and part of the field 'upon part of which the windmill lately stood'. Mill Field was one of the open fields to the north of the parish.

The Hornbuckles were an established Bedfordshire family of millwrights and the low purchase price of £40 meant they could repair the mill. After 5 years the Wilshamstead windmill was presumably in good working order again because Thomas Hornbuckle sold it for £140, making a £100 profit on the sale.

The property being sold included the windmill, a cottage and two selions of land in the open field of Millfield. A selion was a ridge or narrow strip of land of indeterminate size lying between two furrows. It passed through a succession of hands in the latter part of the 18th century.

WINDMILL SUCCESSIVE OWNERS IN LATE 18TH CENTURY

1768   Thomas Hornbuckle of Bedford, Millwright sold to J Kendall of Wilstead, Blacksmith for £140

1773   J Kendall of Wilstead, blacksmith sold to William Dudley of Marston Moretaine, miller for £130

1774   William Dudley of Wilstead, miller sold to Thomas Oliver of Flitwick, yeoman for £140

1778   Thomas Oliver of Flitwick, yeoman sold to Abraham Burr of Wilstead, yeoman for £120

In the enclosure award at the start of the 19th century, the windmill is described as being on the west side of the main road and other historical notes also attribute the site to the west of the road. The enclosure plan shows a tiny drawing of the windmill. From this we can see that the road alignment changed at one point thus causing the discrepancy between the early maps and those of the 19th century.

A second windmill of a later date was located in the fields of Duck End Farm, its approximate site near to the small aerodrome where the footpaths from Duck End Lane and Hooked Lane join.

A number of quern stones used in milling still exist in the village but one in particular was found on the boundary of Village Farm and Duck End Farm near to the site of this second windmill. Although small it is possible that the stone formed

The two sides of a single quern stone found in 'Mill field' near the second windmill site

part of the operation at the second windmill site. This second windmill appears to have been in operation during the middle of the 19th century and probably succeeded the first mill. It is unlikely both windmills were operating at this time.

Both windmills were probably of the post mill type with cloth sails and both were situated in the original open field of Mill Field.

Wilshamstead is often sheltered from some of the worst weather by the Greensand Ridge but on 21st May 1950 Wilshamstead was severely battered by a tornado. The main tornado had arisen following a series of thunderstorms and swept across most of Bedfordshire. Wilstead suffered a great deal of damage from a subsidiary tornado which started in Houghton Conquest and Duck End Farm was particularly badly hit.

All three elements of wood, wind and water are found in a report by the Wilstead correspondent of a gale between Christmas and New Year 1914/15. *The Bedfordshire Times and Independent* reported on January 1 1915:

'The terrific gale of Monday night will long be remembered. The inhabitants of several houses on Cotton End Road were up till 1 and 2am baling out the water, which was knee deep in their homes and over a foot in depth on the main roadway. Similar conditions prevailed in Duck End, the brook overflowed and the lane was impassable. Many fields near Piper's bridge along the main Bedford Road were like a sea. Wood of all kinds was floated out of timber and other yards and even a wheel barrow was carried a good distance. Horses and pigs had to be removed from their usual shelters, the former being up to their bodies in water and the latter nearly washed away. Several of the huge telephone poles with their 58 wires along Luton Road were forced out of the perpendicular.'

An entry for a Wilstead Women's Institute competition for a poem to describe the village in the 1960's prompted Hilda Bourne to include the woods at the very start. She said they always played a part in her childhood games. The tall houses in the rhyme refer to a block of flats near to the Methodist church, which were demolished at the turn of the 21st century.

Once Wilstead Woods but still fields and stiles
A winding road that runs for miles
Past churches, 6 pubs and shops
Can Wilstead boast a few bus stops?.

Standing here by houses tall
Sheds painted white, the village hall
Where singing, talks and playlets cute
Are rendered by our institute.

Hilda Bourne

CHAPTER 12

Bricks and Mortar

The village lost many cottages and older houses in the national trend to modernise in the 1950s and 1960s but despite this loss a number of important buildings still remain to tell their tales.

Join us on a virtual walk around the village as these bricks and mortar impart their history.

Where better place to start than with our own brickworks. Near to the junction of Bedford Road loop and Dane Lane is the house called Dane Oak. This was the home built by the Hebbes family who owned and operated the brickyards. The first brickfield, now a pond, was opened in 1876 and is located to the east of the current A6. The second brickfield was in the fields behind the house and opened around 1886 and is still discernable from Dane Lane today.

Dane Oak Now: 2001

Dane Oak Then

(Reproduced with the kind permission of Bedfordshire and Luton Archives and Records service)

BUILDINGS CONSTRUCTED OF WILSTEAD BRICK STILL IN THE VILLAGE TODAY

- Dane Oak
- Oldest part of current post office
- One of the cottages next to Post Office
- 143 Cotton End Road (previously Tom Wisson's Butchers)
- Ferndale House, Cotton End Road
- Infant School, Cotton End Road
- Infant school mistress house (numbers 80 and 82 Cotton End Road)
- Harry Newman's House (number 77 Cotton End Road)
- Robinson's shop number 10 Bedford Road

Brick workers at Dane Oak

(Reproduced with the kind permission of Enid Wisson)

Charles Hebbes senior and Charles Hebbes junior were farmers in the area and Dane Oak was the centre of activity. The brickworks made a distinctive yellow/brindle brick which can still be seen in a number of properties today.

Behind Dane Oak stood a number of buildings associated with the brickworks. As the hand made bricks needed to be air dried before firing, a drying shed was one these buildings. On 31st July 1919 Charles Hebbes junior gave instructions to Messrs. W and H Peacock to sell the brick making stock, bringing the Wilstead brick industry to a close.

Crossing to the other side of the Bedford Road loop we find the property which was once The White Horse Public House. It was originally a farm operated by

Brick workers at Dane Oak

(Reproduced with the kind permission of Bedfordshire and Luton Archives and Records service)

Inside of drying shed at Dane Oak

(Reproduced with the kind permission of Bedfordshire and Luton Archives and Records service)

'Alfie' Hebbes and was surrounded by milksheds. At this time the Bedford Road loop was the main road and the cows grazed on the land where the A6 now runs.

Part of the farmhouse became a 'front room' pub because of the numbers of workers at the nearby brickworks. It stayed a public house until the early 1990s. Downstairs was a small comfortable room used for drinking and the taproom was in the cellar where the beer was drawn straight from the barrel.

Property that was The White Horse Public House 2001

Travelling further along the loop brings us to the building which was the constabulary police house for the parish. Containing an office at the front, the property was purposely built to house the parish constable. Many houses in parishes were built like this when the responsibility for law and order became a county issue. The area which held the constabulary plaque can still be clearly seen between the upper two windows.

Police House 2001

Entering the village, we reach Duck End Lane and the imposing Duck End Farmhouse, a grade 2 listed building of 18th and 19th century construction. Nearby amongst some late 20th century barn conversions stands an empty cow barn. Thought to have been built about 1800 its 5 bay construction ensures it is also grade 2 listed.

Duck End Farmhouse 2001

Originally owned by the Haynes Park estate, Duck End Farm was purchased at the estate sale in 1914 by Messrs J Newman and Son for £8,032. At the time of the sale the original farmhouse was noted to be at the rear of the main farmhouse. It was sold in 1939 by the Newman family and is currently farmed by the Maskell family.

Strolling back to Bedford Road we see directly opposite, Vicarage Farm. It has also held the name Glebe farm. It is a grade 2 listed building of 17th century construction with some later 19th and 20th century alterations. Alongside the

Vicarage Farm 2001

Cawne Close 2001

property runs Cherry Orchard Lane, an old route that used to connect to Doggetts Lane.

On the opposite side of the road to the farm, the first house we reach is Cawne Close. Contemporary in age to Vicarage Farm it also claims listed status. In the past this smallholding has been owned by the long standing families of Cox, Newman and Simms.

Venturing up to the crossroads we reach the two remaining public houses, The Woolpack and The Red Lion.

Woolpack Now (2001) and Then

(Reproduced with kind permission of Dorothy Houghton)

Beginning with The Woolpack, it was the long standing home of the Crowsley family from the late 19th century until the mid 20th century.

At first a Newland and Nash public house, it was taken over by Wells and Winch Brewery who themselves became part of Green King, the present brewery owners. Before enclosure, the open fields to the north of the parish were grazed by large flocks of sheep and between 1700 and 1739, 22 people in the village listed their occupation as shepherd. The inn sign of the Woolpack reminds us how journeymen used to travel and barter for the fleeces for the wool trade.

Town Close and part of the Woolpack car park was the original site for Wilstead's strangest shaped building. Only having three walls in a triangular shape, the tiny cottage was nicknamed The Cheese Cottage, The Windcutter and The Windsock by various local people.

The cottage had a square living room, triangular kitchen and a tiny triangular room at the top of rickety stairs. It was demolished when property prices rose and the development of Town Close was proposed.

Crossroads with Woolpack, Cheese Cottage and Robinsons grocers

Looking across the road, we can see the Red Lion Public houses, plural, because there are two buildings that have held that name.

The original Red Lion is now a private dwelling that stands back at the end of a small roadway. Grade 2 listed, the building was constructed around 1700 and was originally known as The Bell and then The Compasses before becoming the Red Lion.

The original Red Lion was originally used as a hall house and the early local court sessions and at a later date some of the Poor Law discussions and meetings would be held there.

Our walk now turns from the Crossroads up Church Road. On the right hand side of the road are two thatched cottages of interest.

Red Lions (1960s)

Red Lions 2002

Church Road Cottages Now: 1999
(Reproduced with the kind permission of Barry Huckle)

Church Road Cottages Then

The house on the left of the picture was originally a farriers. The house on the right, now known as Brewley Cottage (a modern name) was originally a pair of smaller cottages built by the farriers for their daughters. Both houses date from around 1800 and are grade 2 listed. In the deeds for the house lies a fascinating tale of how it was mortgaged by later owners to raise funds to build the bake house further down the road.

Near to these properties was the original site of the animal pound. The pound was a fenced area to contain any animals found straying. The Vestry minutes record repairs in 1850 and in 1861 Lord Cartaret of Haynes Park estate sold land along the north side of Church road with the conveyance plan showing the pound abutting Church Road. It later moved to the south east corner of the crossroads where the boundary railings can just be seen in an early postcard which is reproduced later in this chapter. People also recall a later move to the site of the Folly with cows being tied to trees.

At the very top of Church Road on the left we find the most historic building in the village. Church House (sometimes referred to in documents as Church Cottage) has a long and chequered history but has only been a private house since the 1960s.

The first written deeds date to 1572 but it was already in existence before that. Although the date of original construction is unknown it is believed to be a medieval moot hall. Moot is the Saxon term for a gathering of people with a common interest. During the medieval period it is believed the Rector lived in part of the house.

The building was two storeys with the lower level containing rooms which could be let to parishioners and the upper level a single open hall. It was in this hall that the assemblies could be convened for the transaction of business for the proper management of the village. The current owners graciously allowed the authors to examine the roof which still retains its original oak arching beams which would have formed the roof of the open hall.

It is called Church House because the rents and profits from the use of the building and its associated lands, which originally included a field in the parish, were to be employed on the church, churchman or parishoners. It was not owned by the church until later times and was owned by the parish.

During the reformation, Henry VIII confiscated Church House and it was held as part of the manor of Greenwich. It was returned to the parish's ownership in 1572 by Queen Elizabeth I for use as a school and other purposes.

Before tea began to be imported, Church Ales were held in the hall. Church Ales were the forerunners of Church Teas and the Rector and churchwardens held them usually with the expectation of raising a surplus of funds from the collection for a specific project. Within the building would be the plant for brewing the ale and the churchwardens were responsible for the process. The ale was not like the beer of today but was thought to be a sweet beverage made with hops and bitter herbs with low alcoholic content.

Bridal assemblies were held in the hall following weddings at the church and for the poor bride a parish wedding dress was kept at the church house for their use.

In 1723 a parliamentary statute allowed churchwardens to hire out buildings for the lodging and employment of the poor. Under this Act, the workhouse of Wilshamstead was established in Church House under a Vestry resolution dated 19th October 1796. The Wilshamstead overseers accounts record some of the inmates and the masters and matrons.

By 1838, the building was divided into cottages and the Guardians of the Poor of the Bedford Union sold these to Richard Quenby, local farmer, for £34. In 1839, it was sold again for £28 before being conveyed to Reverend Passy and a number of parish officers on 10 March 1841.

Church House continued to be used as rented cottages but by the second world war it was used to store all the paper gathered by the village for the war effort.

By 1959, it was abandoned and was under threat of being turned into a car park for the church. In 1962, it was sold into the private ownership of Mr and Mrs John Pope who converted it into a modern dwelling. A number of domestic items

Church Cottage 1999

(Reproduced with the kind permission of Barry Huckle)

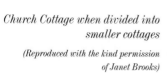

Church Cottage when divided into smaller cottages

(Reproduced with the kind permission of Janet Brooks)

1960s restoration back and front
(Reproduced with the kind permission of Dianne and John Pope)

including an old wooden spoon were found when the wattle and daub walls were replaced. A large igloo style communal oven on the outside wall was preserved within the fabric of the restored building. This bread oven had been used by poor villagers for many years.

Adjacent to the house was the associated barn and before the sale the hand drawn hearse anciently used for village funerals was kept there. It now resides in the coach house at the vicarage awaiting restoration.

Passing through the gates and into the churchyard, the footpath takes us past the church and along the edge of the vicarage property.

A grand Vicarage stood on the same site as the present Vicarage. It was part Georgian and part Victorian.

In 1710 the Vicarage buildings consisted of 2 parlours, a hall, a paved kitchen, a dairy, a pitched brew-house, and a cellar. In addition it had 4 bed chambers and a garret. Outside stood a wood house, stable ,hay barn, coach house, game larder, tool shed, and the stables. The stables still exist on the grounds today. The servants quarters were built on the north side of the vicarage but this was described as 'a rag tag', not very well built building. By late 19th century, there was a carved wooden staircase, which lead to the upstairs rooms. Downstairs included the drawing room, dining room, the scullery, pantry, china pantry, kitchens and the servants back staircase. To the left of the hallway was another room that may well have been used as a study and adjacent was the Parish room. The Parish room was used as a meeting room for the parishioners and it was also accessible from the back of the Vicarage.

Over the years the condition of the Vicarage deteriorated and regrettably, the demolition of the

View of the Victorian vicarage from the lawn
(Reproduced with the kind permission of Sandra Whitaker)

noble vicarage took place in 1969. Understandably, for many of the local people it was difficult to comprehend why such a beautiful building was not worthy of restoration and preservation by the Diocese and this is still cause for comment today.

Collins & Sons built the present Vicarage in 1972. The Vicarage was consecrated on 22 March 1975 by the then Bishop of Bedford.

During the 600 years from 13th to 19th century the building was known as the Rectory because the incumbent of the parish received tithes from the landowners. Once this practice stopped the building became a Vicarage as the clergyman receives a stipend.

As we exit the footpath into Vicarage Lane we are greeted by grade 2 listed Little Church Farm. Built around 1700, it was farmed until the 1960s. It then became one of only three centres at that time for the International League for the Protection of Horses. People still recall it as the Donkey Sanctuary.

Little Church Farm 2001

At the bottom where the lane joins the original line of the Luton Road, used to stand Mrs Fairy's railway carriage.

Turning left onto the small loop we catch our first glimpse of the house locally referred to as eyebrow cottage. A grade 2 listed 18th century building, the thatched arches that give it its nickname were added in the 19th century. The property was the home of the Kendall family who were wheelwrights. In 1914, William Kendall extended the cottage holdings by buying an area of land to the north of the cottage from the Haynes Park estate. On 29 November 1916, the entire wheelwrights stock was catalogued by W H Peacock for auction. Amongst the items were a brickwork forge and bellows

Mrs Fairy and Mrs Stokes
(Reproduced with the kind permission
of Brian Crouch)

Eyebrow Cottage 2001

Two members of the Kendall
family stand outside.

(Reproduced with the kind permission of Janet Brooks)

Demolished cottages, blacksmiths house (middle distance) & pound railings on right hand side before phone box

(Reproduced with the kind permission of Bedfordshire and Luton Archives and Records service)

valued at £1–10s and a pair of timber cart wheels at 3 shillings.

From here we walk back to the crossroads passing the sites of cottages demolished in 1972, the animal pound and the blacksmiths house .

Turning into Cotton End Road we can see Manor House. This was originally a coaching inn called The Pear Tree Inn and local rumour says it was the original base for the manor house but its construction has only been dated to the 19th century. It is believed an earlier name was Rosemont and it was the Old Manor House Hotel before becoming the home of Manor Antiques. An old photograph of the property can be found in the Name Game chapter.

The Old Manor House name is likely to stem from a previous ownership by a Lord of the Manor and may have referred to an earlier building on the site. A remaining wall from the 17th Century on the right hand side of the property is the original wall of an old barn.

Two long gone public houses are The Nags Head and The Chequers. The Nags Head stood where the bungalows stand to the right of Dines Close, The Chequers stood next door to the Post Office. Constructed of Wilstead brick The Chequers was demolished a few years ago and the bricks were reclaimed and used in the construction of the three millennium village signs.

In 1926 Alfred Charles Redman purchased the Chequers from the Brewers Simson & Co from Baldock Herts. It was a small building with a narrow entrance and two rooms at the front each side of a small wooden panelled passage. The cellar was to the right hand side and the room at the back was used for snooker type games. It had a well in the back yard.

From right to left: Post Office, The Chequers, Cox butchers, The Nags Head and Doras Stores, Cotton End Road

(Reproduced with the kind permission of Margaret Pearce)

Further down Cotton End Road we find The Elephant and Castle Public House. Now a private house, its construction is thought to be about 1700. Its long low style of construction gave rise to a saying 'If you've got cold feet, you'll soon warm 'em up walking the length of The Elephant and Castle'.

Originally a beer house run by Herbert Masters and Ethel Mary Masters, the last landlords took over in 1939. Jessie and Sidney West kept it until it closed in the late 1960s.

Elephant and Castle now: 2002

There was no room for a counter and it was one of the few remaining old fashioned pubs where the drinks were brought to you direct from the cellar. The interior had polished old benches as seats and bumpy tiled floors.

In 1937 a stonemason lodged here whilst renovating the church and created an unusual fireplace. It has been described as 'scintillating with light and colour it is a glittering mosaic of pieces of mirror-glass, fragments of gay pottery and china and brilliant polished stones.' In the centre of it is a plaque as a memento to King George VI with his queen.

Elephant and Castle then
(Reproduced with the kind permission of Bedford Central Library)

As well as the usual drinks, the pub sold barley wines. Only three glasses were allowed or else the knees would start to give way! As one local recalled the 'head was clear as a bell but feet just wouldn't go!' The Elephant and Castle later served Chitling suppers (stomach of pig turned inside out and fried) in the function room at the back.

The Rechabite friendly society in Wilstead who met at the Wesleyan Chapel were total abstainers from alcohol. At one time the owner of the Elephant and Castle wanted to erect a sign at the cross roads as he felt he was off the beaten track but the Rechabites objected vigorously.

Nearby is a building of Wilstead brick, the property referred to by many as Harry Newman House.

The Ancient Order of Foresters Wilstead branch dates back to 1866 when Wilstead, in the Northampton District was granted dispensation to open the court 'Unity'. It was granted to Edward Travis of the Elephant & Castle

Harry Newman House 2001

Public House, which stayed its meeting place until 1895 when the court moved to the Woolpack public house. The officers as a form of identification wore sashes and a banner and horns formed part of the regalia.

Unity was a successful Court with its members increasing from 35 to a total of 288 in 1905. The Foresters provided a mutual insurance scheme for its members and gave assistance to those in need. It flourished until the National Insurance Act came into place after the Second World War. By 1939 numbers had declined to 173.

In 1949 the generosity of Mrs Oliver who lived in Bristol but whose family roots were in Wilstead made it possible for the Court to have its own Courthouse. Mrs Oliver gifted a property in memory of her father whose house it had been. This courthouse became known locally as the Harry Newman House and is still referred to as that today. The male members of the Court undertook repairs to the property before it was opened according to ritual and toasted to its future success. The courts success was confirmed in the Foresters' Miscellany Court and District News of 1963 when it was described as 'one of the most live Courts in the District'. The property is now a private house.

Reaching an opening in the vista of Cotton End Road we can see across the fields to Manor Farm. Probably the original site of the main manor base after sale of the

Manor by Elstow Abbey, its current buildings date to the 16th century with later 19th century alterations. The farmhouse and its granary barn are grade 2 listed. Thomas Armstrong who was woodsman to Lord Cartaret, used to go up into the granary to read his

Manor Farm 2001

Cooper family outside Ivy Cottage, now Long Thatch

(Reproduced with the kind permission of Malcolm Terry)

Long Thatch 1999

(Reproduced with the kind permission of Barry Huckle)

bible and the book remained on the rafters for many years after he died.

In the Chapel End area is Long Thatch, which is believed to have been built of lathe and plaster in the 17th century. Owned by Haynes Park Estate until 1914 it was known as Ivy Cottage because of its ivy clad walls. It later became known as Homestead before being named Long Thatch in the 1980s.

At the time of the sale in 1914, it had a large kitchen garden and orchard and was used as two cottages. The Cooper family purchased it and converted it into a single house, adding barns at the sides. In 1941 it was split again into two cottages and remained this way until the formal conversion of both cottages and the barns into one house in the 1980s. A well in the front garden provided the drinking water for the cottage but is now only for decorative purposes.

Passing down Cotton End Road we come to Northwoood Lane. A small holding on the right hand side was owned by the Jellis family. Now the site of modern houses, the original farmhouse was used as a cow shed before its final demolition. Ray Nettleship can recall driving the cattle up the stairs to shelter.

Jellis Farmhouse circa 1962.

(Reproduced with the kind permission of Bedfordshire and Luton Archives and Records Service)

Crossing over Cotton End Road we reach Ivy Lane. The ownership of properties here changed dramatically when 11 cottages were sold by Haynes Park estate in 1914. A pleasant walk along the length of this lane takes you from the first of the 11, a thatched cottage on the corner of Cotton End road now called Spindle Cottage to the eleventh at the very top now number 26 Ivy Lane.

Many in between have changed but one worthy of note is Compton Cottage. It was formerly part of Freddie Smith's slaughterhouse holdings and we are told was named after a family pet dog, Compton. Grade 2 listed it dates to the 18th century. The coach lamps still by the front door in 2002 are believed to be from an early vehicle used by the family to deliver milk.

Compton Cottage and coach lamps just under the porch eaves 2001

Towards the far end of Cotton End Road once stood a building with a chequered history. It was originally a public house called the Carpenters Arms and its deeds – now in the local records office – date back to 1730. It later became a smallholding of 17.5 acres known as Red House Farm. A number of sad tales of events happening to the owners are still told in the village giving strength to the rumours that the property

Cotton End Farm 2001

Barn 2002

Cotton End Manor Farm 2002

Cotton End Manor Farm in 1898

(Reproduced with the kind permission of Bedfordshire and Luton Archives and Records Service)

was haunted. It was demolished in the late 20th century and the site is now occupied by 148 Cotton End Road and The Stables Equestrian Centre.

At the top of Elms Lane stands Cotton End Farm. The farmhouse dates back to the 17th century although changes were made in the 18th and 19th centuries. Grade 2 listed it was purchased from the Haynes Park Estate by Rudd Green. The Green family still farm there today. An earlier name for the farm was Potters End Farm.

The farmhouse kitchen contains a large inglenook fireplace with an original brick lined bread oven to one side. Another feature of note is the barn that stands adjacent to Cotton End Road. The barn was used to store sheaves of wheat and corn which were brought into the barn by horse and cart. To enable both horse and cart to fit, an area was specially constructed to take the horse and this can be seen jutting out of the side today. Sadly in the late 20th century a car demolished part of this feature and it had to be rebuilt.

Taking a pleasant stroll down Elms Lane, we reach Cotton End Manor Farm. Owned by the Whitbread Estate, it is tenanted by the Seamark family who also have a successful sheep dog display team.

This farm is likely to have been directly associated with and could have originated from the medieval assarting with main periods of clearance and boundary creation in 12th and 13th century. Some of the current field boundaries have been on these lines since this early time.

Rectilinear earthworks in a pasture near to the farmhouse are thought to indicate the original manorial complex. It is known an early farmhouse burnt down on this site and was replaced nearby with the current building in the 17th century.

It is believed that John Bunyan visited the farm as a child with his father and grandfather to see George Edwards who was in residence. Circa 1618, Edwards described himself as a Yeoman and the house was of a hall style with a large kitchen cum dining room. The Edwards family are commemorated in plaques in All Saints Church.

The farmhouse was restored by Mr S Whitbread in 1911 and is thought to be the original seat for the Westcotts Manor. Both Manor and farmhouse were purchased by the Whitbread family.

Venturing into Littleworth, we reach The Rose Public House, which has been a private property since the 1990s .

The building on the left of the pub was erected as a clubhouse by steam engine railway enthusiasts Wilstead and District Vintage Machinery Society. They later moved to Summerfields farm at Haynes turn and became the Beds Engineering Club and then Bedford Model Engineering Society.

Another small enthusiast group the Rusty Iron Club sometime met at The Rose but now usually group at the Bowls club.

Other important buildings still remain and they have been covered in other chapters. However as housing developments and change occur, the face of the village will also continue to change, and this is reflected in the following poem.

The Rose 1960s
(Reproduced with the kind permission of Enid Wisson)

The Rose, 1980s
(Reproduced with the kind permission of Janet Brooks)

The Rose 2002

ARRIVEDERCI WILSTEAD

Resigned to what now lies in store,
A time when you will be no more
A village; more an urban sprawl,
A place by builders held in thrall
Who standing firmly at the helm,
Will build for us an urban realm.
An ever growing conurbation
Heeding not our consternation.
West of Luton road today,
Tomorrow nearby Whitworth Way?
And then the odd field here and there
By which time nobody will care
A damn for what the future holds
Or whats been planned or built or sold.
The Parish Council may decry
This concept and give reasons why
It may not happen; but how they try
They are impotent; just like you or I.
Farewell then Wilstead, your destiny awaits
Submergence in a culture of Identikit estates

JIM McCARTHY APRIL 2000

CHAPTER 13

Down Memory Lane

The history of the daily life of the village lies with the people of the parish and the events that have taken place. Sometimes, only the recollections and memories of local people can show how times have changed.

The authors of this book are indebted to all the kind people who freely gave their time, their stories and their wonderful collection of anecdotes to show how life used to be.

A number of the tales have been passed on from family generation to generation and others are first hand experience. Let these stories take you down Wilstead's memory lane and share the bygone days. Where better place to start than those memories of childhood spanning the last century.

Children found pleasure in the simplest forms of play. In the 1920s, it was common practice for young lads to call in at the slaughterhouse in Ivy Lane and ask Freddie Smith for a pig's bladder which made a great football. The boys would spend hours playing football on the grass at Luton Road and often kicked a ball to and from school in Church Road.

When they were not kicking a football, they found other amusements. In the 1940s when no one was looking, particularly the local bobby, Mr Jacquest (known as Mr Jakes), they would attempt to shoot the china cups from

China cups on poles outside the Red Lion

(*Reproduced with kind permission of Sandra Whitaker*)

the tops of the telegraph poles with their catapults.

Another game was a version of the ever-popular child's game 'knock down ginger.' Near to the Wesleyan Chapel in Chapel Lane used to stand a row of three cottages. The young boys tied the door knobs of all the three houses together with string, knocked on all of the doors and then swiftly ran off. Can you imagine the commotion when all the doors tried to open at the same time? Even worse was pushing stinging nettles through holes in the outside toilets of cottages, which stood at the entrance where Dines Close is now.

One gentleman can recall how in the 1940s he and other young boys from Littleworth were reprimanded by the local bobby, Mr Jacquest for no fault of their own. This happened when a group of young lads from Bedford decided to visit Littleworth. They played shooting games with their catapults and broke one of the widows of St Paul's church. Their curiosity overtook them and they were soon in the church dressing-up in the choirboy cassocks before parading in the Littleworth area holding the holy cross. This was reported to Mr Jacquest who assumed it was the Littleworth lads and fined each of them even though they were not there. To this day no one believes that the Reverend Pollard was ever convinced of their innocence.

The girls had more gentle pastimes. One lady has fond memories of Mrs Whitworth who used to sit near to the french doors of the Victorian vicarage and delighted in telling her stories. When St Pauls church in Littleworth was built many recall the Reverend Whitworth (secretly known as Dicki by the local children) riding his bike to the church every Sunday and Mrs Whitworth being pulled along in a wicker type chair on wheels.

The ponds were a magnet for all children, whatever time of the year. Summer hours were spent paddling in either the pond at the far end of Doggetts Lane or the pond with an island in the middle, sited where Whitworth Way stands today. During the severe cold winters skating took place on the pond near to the Infants school in Cotton End Road. On one occasion one little boy by the name of Wag was not lucky. He was paddling one pleasant day when he lost his brand new shoe. He ordered his dog to fetch it but to no avail and he knew his mother would be furious. For the following month he was sent to school with the remaining new shoe on one foot and a plimsoll on the other.

Scrumping in orchards was always popular before settling down to a game of marbles or whips and tops. Often, when the apples had been harvested the Reverend Pollard would arrive at Sunday school with a basket of apples as a treat. The children would pick watercress for the family to enjoy at teatime. This grew abundantly in the clear water of the ditches at Cotton End Farm and Duck End Farm.

The parish magazine of March 1900 shows how the children marched through the village singing Rule Britannia whilst collecting for the widows and orphans of the South African war. This followed the arrival of the news of the victory at Kimberley Paardeberg when the parish bells were rung in celebration.

Elizabeth King came to live in the village as a child in 1830 and in 1898 her memories were recorded in a newspaper article. Her story provides a vivid description of Thomas Armstrong who was woodsman to Lord Carteret 'he was dressed in leather coat, breeches and gaiters.....his style of living consisted of 2 basins of milk a day, one morning and one evening and he used to carry his lunch with him to the wood in the form of a wedge of cheese and a piece of bread in his pockets, with a 2 quart leather bottle of beer....and the wallet into which he put his tools carried across his shoulders on his way to work.'

Lord Carteret and his family owned Haynes Park Estate and stories have been passed down of when horse drawn carriages with smart horses came down the carriageway drive to Wilshamstead. When a son of the family came home from India he found the carriageway drive all lit up with lanterns to welcome him back.

At a later date, the gate to the carriageway drive had its own gatekeepers, Mr and Mrs Chapman who lived in one of the lodge houses. As you face the gate, the lodge houses stood on the left hand side of the drive with the front doors onto the drive. A modern house now occupies the site.

The Chapmans were in charge of locking the gates each evening and unlocking them in the morning. On one occasion during the Second World War, the army was undertaking manoeuvres in the woods and wanted access for a tank. The Chapmans had locked the gates and would not open them and so the tank rolled over the gates knocking them flat.

Both adults and children have spent many days in Wilstead Wood. There are vivid memories of the woods with hedgerows, lilac bushes, bluebells, primroses and violets. Children would take jam sandwiches and a bottle of lemonade or water and play until dusk. Sometimes wild strawberries and beechnuts were for the picking. Going primrosing meant gathering bunches of primroses and tying them with wool. These could be sold for a copper or ha'penny, just enough to afford a Tom Thumb toffee bar. Children would also go wooding. Taking a pram or a home-made stretcher, they would load it with bits of dead wood for the fires back home.

From the very top of the woods some children from Littleworth could actually hear their mothers calling them at teatime to return home from the woods. At Easter they would be occupied with rolling hard-boiled eggs down the hill before finding and eating them.

The village was supplied by a number of shops and trades people and these characters and buildings formed an important part of the everyday routine.

In the centre of the village, the noise and smell from the blacksmith's at the crossroads was familiar to many. One day Mr Wesley Rogers a baker from Haynes called in at the smithy because his horse needed shoeing. Whilst his father wasn't looking, the blacksmith's son painted the horse with red stripes. Arthur Mastin, the blacksmith, had to work extremely hard to clean the horse but despite his best efforts the horse still appeared pink. Luckily the customer did not notice.

Further up Church Road was the bake house. The children often called in on their way to and from the school. In the middle of the day some of them would share a small 2d loaf for their lunch. The baker, Mr Edgar Richardson would often give a twisted plait of hot bread to the first child to arrive at the shop in the morning.

*Edgar's son Ken Richardson
making deliveries at
The Bell Cotton End*

(*Reproduced with the kind permission
of Miriam Langford*)

Many families can remember when they would take their Sunday dinner to be cooked in the ovens at the bake house for a small charge of one penny plus an extra ha'penny for Yorkshire puddings.

Mischievous boys would pull on the springs at the back of the bread buggy to try and hold it back. Edgar Richardson would let the lads play along for a while but when he had had enough he would flick his whip backwards and catch the boys with a slight touch and they would then let go. The whip did not hurt them.

Before the advent of the milkmen of today, milk was delivered largely by two village families. They used to take the milk churns round and people would come out and fill their jugs. Luton and Bedford Road and the crossroads area was served by the Sharpe family with some deliveries in Cotton End Road. One member widely remembered is Hedley Sharpe, the son of Arthur Mastin Sharpe who owned Briar Bank Farm in Luton Road. Hedley is well remembered for walking and cycling with his feet at 'to to 2' The farmhouse is now a residential property and the farmland later became the Briar Bank Mobile Home Park.

Hedley milked the cows in the cowshed on the site of the current Briar Bank Social Club and cycled around the village with large milk churns on both sides of his handlebars. When milk bottles came into use, he used a trade bike with 2 crates of milk bottles in front of him plus three bags of bottles on either side of the handlebars!

The village locals knew Arthur Mastin Sharpe as Darti Sharpe. One of his nieces could not say the name Arthur as a child, so he gained the nickname Darti. The

'Darti' Sharpe and his wife

(*Reproduced with the kind permission of Miriam Langford*)

farm locally became known as Darti Sharpe's dairy farm. When delivering milk he was heard calling, "I'm here, I'm here, my milk beats all the beer."

Eva Bozier (nee Taylor) from Ivy Lane delivered milk in Cotton End Road and Littleworth. Eva did not have her own dairy farm but she purchased the milk and made her deliveries by bicycle whilst singing on her rounds.

Memories from the 1920s and 1930s of butchers in the village include Freddie Smith at the slaughterhouse in Ivy Lane, slaughtering sheep and pigs and nephew Cyril Taylor calling at people's houses to kill their pigs. The owners of the pig would shave it and Cyril would cut it up. If Mr Cox, the butcher on Cotton End road ran out of skewers he would cross the road to cut some twigs from the hedge. Later in the 1930s to 1940s an advert for Mr Ives said, 'Meat of merit is the kind you deserve on your table, the kind you get from H. R. Ives'.

In the early days of the Post Office in the 19th century they never found it difficult distributing mail to the right address even when a letter was received marked only with a recipients name and 'Near Post Office, Wilstead.' It was soon delivered because there were not many houses. At a similar time a lady who lived in Ivy Lane asked a young boy to write a letter for her. He duly obeyed and when he asked for the address for the envelope she replied "London." She thought this was sufficient, as she believed London was as small as Wilstead!

Early transport was via carrier horse and cart. Mr Joseph Finding was one of the carriers in Wilshamstead for approximately 28 years until 1938. In an article by Gladys Toll, Mr Finding was described as a Wesleyan preacher for the Sunday school with a reputation as a rhymester as he would recite a little poetry during the services.

One day, apparently, a lady asked Mr Finding to lend her some money. "I've left me purse in me old skirt at home", she said. However, as she stepped down from the cart the old skirt fell down from beneath her best one!

Occasional trips to the seaside required careful planning. Mr Hedge told locals of a trip that had been arranged in the 1920s. The plan was to get to the coast by train from St Johns Railway Station in Bedford. As they had to get from Wilshamstead to the station, the party hired Joseph Finding to take them. Joseph's horse was known for having a peculiar habit. It would run for 200 yards before it would get breathless and then it would decide to walk for the next 100 yards. They set off early in the morning to try to avoid any problems this peculiar habit may cause. However, even with an early start, when they arrived at Bedford they saw the train passing under the bridge beneath them. Joseph's pragmatic remark was, "we weren't far behind" and this phrase has been remembered in several families.

Transport was scarce in the village in the early 20th century. In the 1930s Mr Wolveridge had an Isotta Francini car and up to 10 children crammed into this car at the crossroads and drove up to St Paul's Church at Littleworth. At times when the car was not running too well, children at the time can remember pushing the car to Littleworth instead.

Between the wars many women from Wilshamstead worked in the Cardington hangers on the airships. The task they were doing was called doping which

R101 crew

(Reproduced with kind permission of Dorothy Cooper)

involved covering the linen with a chemical that produced the silver colouring on the airships. A number of people recalled how this particular fabric made wonderful curtains for the home.

However, when an audit enquiry was held an inspector went out to make house to house calls. The appearance of the village changed overnight as all the houses removed their curtains for fear of being caught. Supposedly, department store Braggins in Bedford, sold out of curtains that weekend! Sadly, history recalls the devastating news when the crew on the R101 airship crashed in France on 5th October 1930 on its way to India. It was a sad day for the village as Mr A J Richardson from the bakery family was a crewman on board.

The owners at Cotton End Farm have witnessed some comical characters over time including the amusing behaviour of individuals who after a few beverages at The Rose Public House would later dance round the water pump at the top of Elms Lane before completing their journey home. This provided great entertainment from the top landing window of the farmhouse!

Characters often become timeless because of some comical or interesting personality or event.

Old Henry was a well-spoken man from an aristocratic background but he had chosen to live his life as a tramp. His real name was William Cunningham and he lived in a field at Herrings Green before moving to Cotton End village in the 1940s. Old Henry read his newspaper with glasses, which had one lens in them. When asked a question about the articles he would remark, "Nothing to interest you". Mrs Green from Cotton End Farm would prepare meals for him but despite his lifestyle he would never walk in front of the pigsty with his food, he would always walk behind it.

A local farm worker named Long Wil lived near the Mission Hall. He helped out on Hanley's farm (Cotton End Manor Farm) and got his name because of his long and thin physique. Similarly, Mr Frank Burr was popularly called Pussycat Burr and it is believed that this is because of his whiskers. One man who lived in a 'road mender type' caravan in the field next to The Rose Public House was known as Old Caravan Joe.

Mrs Jessie Gilbert used to teach the piano. One particular day a surveyor called at her property and asked, "Where are the stairs?" to which she replied, "Can't you see it's a thundering bungalow" and shut the door. The tale of her reply spread in no time at all.

'Sally' Cambers is remembered because of his well-known phrase. He used to cycle from Wilshamstead to Elstow and on arrival he always checked the time against the church clock. He was convinced that he had made the journey from Wilshamstead to Elstow in '5 minutes less than no time.' This was because the Elstow church clock was five minutes slower than Wilstead church clock.

Harry Crowsley was remembered by many but particularly by a group of young lads who spent many a Saturday afternoon huddled together in the hen run behind the Woolpack Public House. "Don't make no noise and I'll leave you a crate in the hen run," Harry would say. The boys were delighted as they passed the time away drinking the beer!

Later, Harry hit the headlines in the 1960s when he retired. The locals purchased a barometer for his retirement gift and when it was presented to him they discovered the plaque read 'on the occasion of their engagement'. The plaque was promptly corrected to read 'retirement.'

We cannot forget to mention Mrs Wilson who was the 'lollipop lady' for the children at the crossroads before the bypass. She would throw the lollipop at passing cars who drove too fast through the village and if children missed their bus to Elstow school she would flag down a car and ensure that the children were given a lift to school.

The second world war was a difficult time for all and there are plenty of memories of the war years. In the village shops, margarine was sold in 2 and 4-ounce portions and when it was not available the next best thing for greasing was liquid paraffin. Tea had to be weighed and sugar was sold in blue bags. There were tins of fish called 'snoek' and dried egg powders. Hairgrips and make-up were not available so flour was used as face powder and soot made great toothpaste.

Many would try to swap an egg ration voucher for corn feed for chickens. Others can remember 'gleaning' in the cornfield behind the village hall where pieces of corn left after the main harvest could be picked up and used to feed for the chickens. Families who grew their own fruits were able to bottle the fruits in kilner jars in preparation for the Christmas season.

As meat was rationed there was a high demand for rabbit meat during the war years. People went rabbitting and one day as many as 30 rabbits were caught on a shoot at Cotton End Farm.

At one time a bomb flew over the houses and landed in one of Cotton End Manor farm's fields apparently making a good sized hole although luckily it did not cause any damage to the property. On another occasion, the Green family at Cotton End Farm was sitting in the kitchen enjoying their cocoa when dust shook off the beams. They later learnt this had been caused by a small bomb in Elstow.

Several incendiary devices were dropped in the field to the right of the carriageway drive and sticker bombs were dropped in the Dane Lane area. Farmers had to leave implements in the fields to prevent aircraft from landing. The Wilstead air raid precaution headquarters were established in the Manor House with smaller centres at a chicken hut on Cotton End Road near Ivy Lane and at Dane Lane. Lads aged 12 to 13 years would act as ARP (air raid precaution) messengers. One messenger had to cycle up and down to the Cotton End Road centre whilst another would go to Dane Lane. The messengers were given a colour of the warning, for example if the air raid warning was red this signified that they only had 15 minutes to relay the messages before the sirens sounded. Messages also had to be relayed to Tom Foggarty, the lieutenant of the Home Guard who lived in a coffin-shaped house near to Dora's store and Mr Owers who acted as a warden sounding his whistle to warn the locals to fetch their gas masks. Mr Owers lived in the old bake house next door to the Elephant and Castle Public House.

Mr Douglas Wolveridge, the lay reader was responsible for transporting iron railings to the war offices in Cumberland Avenue in London so the metal could be used for scrap. A local lad can recall the day he accompanied Mr Wolveridge. Whilst in London they suddenly heard guns firing and the sound of sirens. Mr Wolveridge turned to the young lad and commented, "we're alright, especially if there is a bombshell, bombs never strike twice." He must have been very confident because his vehicle was the only one parked in sight during such dangerous times.

Certain incidents that occurred are reminiscent of the television series Dad's Army! One evening a gentleman living in the village rushed into his friend's house and exclaimed he was alarmed because bullets were being fired in Luton Road. Soon afterwards another friend came in flustered. He exclaimed in a stutter that whilst he was cleaning his gun he had accidentally ejected the bullets. Unbeknown to him a bullet had shot a hole through his own front door, near to the Manor House and had fired down Luton Road.

The war shaped the daily life of the children of the village. The air raid sirens did not frighten them but in fact they stood outside their homes to see the searchlights if they got the chance. Children helped the community by collecting paper and newspapers for the war effort and stored them in the abandoned Church House. The stacks of newspaper were great places to play hide and seek and their energy levels were certainly strengthened by the cod liver oil and orange juice they were given at school.

In 1939 a group of 103 evacuee children, mainly from Cricklewood came to stay in the village. Mr Porter from Porters Garage in Luton Road acted as the evacuee-billeting officer and was responsible for ensuring that the children had settled happily in their new homes in the country. Others have remembered the boiler at the vicarage that heated water and was then used to bath the younger evacuee children – 'the little blessings that were not so fresh!' Only one evacuee never returned to London and chose to remain in the village marrying a local lad.

A visitor to the village who went on to become famous was Diana Dors. Staying at Duck End in the late 1940s for a short while, an eyewitness recalls how she opened the door in a red satin dressing gown and others recall seeing her in her yellow sports car.

Every day creatures such as rabbits often find their way into a tale. A story handed down is of how the members of Haynes Park Estate provided soup and rabbit to the needy and poor of the village in the late 19th Century. The rabbit was presumably surplus from an organised shooting, but the village had in it's time a few poachers. One of the tricks used to catch pheasants was to soak grain in alcohol so that once eaten the birds would be so drowsy they would fall off the trees and apparently a delicious pie could be made with sparrows, known by some as spadger pie.

Once when the rooks near the church became pests, people asked Reverend Pollard if they would be allowed to shoot at the nests. He replied, "The Lord sent rooks for a purpose, they eat the wild worm you know out of the lamb; I couldn't consider you shooting these rooks at any price." The locals duly obeyed and the rooks were safe.

An ongoing legend is the tale of an underground passage leading from Manor House to Manor Farm in Cotton End Road. Fascinating as it sounds there has been no physical evidence of this and nobody seems to know where the rumour started.

We shall leave memory lane with a story that made the newspapers. At the rear of St Paul's Church Littleworth was a brick building where the large copper for heating water for social events was stored. In the 1930s it was stolen and the thief rode off with it on his bike. The local bobby apprehended the criminal and the next day the newspaper headlines read:

COPPER CATCHES COPPER COPPER!

CHAPTER 14

Wilstead – The Third Millennium

Time Capsule burial ceremony 2000, Joan Wheeler chairman of Parish Council

As we enter the third millennium the parish is poised on the edge of great change. The Oakley Grange housing development on Luton Road is being built on a field that was once cow pasture.

The proposed development of the second world war bomb factory site at Elstow Storage Depot will change the shape of the parish with a completely new village being introduced. Suggested names include Wixam, Upper Wilstead and Miller Green. History will tell what it will become.

The re-alignment of part of the A6 trunk road will mean the old section of road referred to as the Bedford Loop will disappear.

Yet this is history in the making and in time it will become an event of the past.

To mark the turn of the new millennium, the parish council buried a millennium time capsule. It contains laminated reports and photographs from all the village organisations showing Wilstead as it was in the year 2000. Vacuum sealed in a box especially designed and constructed by Michael Maskell of Duck End Farm, it was buried on 30 December 2000 for future generations to enjoy.

To end right up to date we must record the celebrations of the Golden Jubilee. From 1st to the 3rd of June 2002, Wilstead celebrated 50 years of Queen Elizabeth II reign with events including a fete and fun day on the recreation ground, a fun day at Briar Bank, a concert in the Methodist Church and a flower festival, arts display and songs of praise in All Saints Church. The festivities all ended with a

Briar Bank Fun Day
3 June 2002 opened by
Mayor of Bedford

very well attended evening village picnic with fireworks on the recreation ground. A week later a barbeque and disco was held at the Bowls Club.

Barry Huckle of the village jubilee working group captured the spirit in the July 2002 parish newsletter by saying 'I am sure you will agree that it was great to have such a buzz in the village with so many people determined to celebrate as a community. Long may it continue'.

APPENDIX 1

Vicars of Wilshamstead

Dates of institution where known

1235	Richard de Leire
	Robert (surname not recorded)
28 May 1275	Robert de Cumbes
1308	Richard de Edelesbio
21 September 1308	Peter son of Hugh Luffenham
1377	John Clerk
1404	John Lucas
1 October 1404	John Wrattyng
1441	Adam Dooet
26 February 1455	John Grace
21 December 1461	Richard Hyndeman
27 April 1462	Henry Lewy
29 May 1466	John Passewater / John Purser
5 September 1492	Richard Purser
5 November 1524	Thomas Harward
16 January 1559	Peter Whyte
18 January 1574	Thomas Aldrich
8 August 1598	Robert Risley
6 November 1623	Edward Riseley
1662	William Wells
2 April 1687	Samuel Richardson
25 March 1730	John Gay
23 December 1745	Barnard Garnett
12 June 1754	Megison Newton
13 July 1780	William Pickering
26 November 1782	Thomas Bedford
24 September 1793	Anthonyy Dauvert
24 September 1815	Thomas Bedford
27 June 1816	Frederic Pawsey
1843	Frederic Charles George Passy
1871	John Heyrick Macaulay
1884	Arthur Wollaston Rose
1887	Richard Charles Whitworth
1930	H P Pollard
1949	P W Shepherd Smith (Curate in Charge)
1950	Charles Buck
1953	Alfred John Watkins
1955	William E Napier Munn
1964	William H Stanger
1970	M John Hill

1978	Martin John Banister (Curate in Charge)
1980	Martin John Banister (Rector of Wilshamstead and Houghton Conquest)
1990	Roderick Palmer
11 January 2002	Stephen J Toze

APPENDIX 2

Known Schoolmasters and Teachers

EARLY SCHOOLMASTERS

1689–1820	Kendall
	Joseph Millar
	Francis Wingrave (buried 1758)
1821	Robert Miller
Unknown	Mefibosheth Knight
1840	Abraham Burr
Unknown	Herbert Carrier
Unknown	W G Boole

INFANT SCHOOL

1876	Eliza Boston – Mistress
1877	Mary Ann Henshawe (later Pearce)
1904	Fanny Plumb – Mistress
1928	Ms Brown – Teacher
1930s	Lilian Whyley – Mistress
1930s	Margaret Daniels – Asst
1946	Muriel Cook – Mistress
1946	Ms Holland – Teacher
1946	Miss Cressessent – Teacher
1948	Hilda Bourne – Asst

WILSHAMSTEAD NATIONAL SCHOOL

1847	Abraham Burr
1850	James Herbert – Master, Elizabeth Griffin – Mistress
1869	James Herbert – Master, Charlotte Herbert – Mistress
1873	Joseph Carrier – Master
1881	Frederick Hampton – Master
1891	Georgina Hampton – Teacher
1903	Edith Wood
1921	Edith Lodge – Mistress
1928	Ms Hughes – Mistress
1929	Ms Kingston – Teacher

1930s	Ms Brewster –Mistress
1948	Miss Hickling – Mistress
1948	Miss Stevens –Supply Teacher
1948	Miss Daniels (moved to Top School from Infants school)
1956	E M Rimes – Mistress

WILSHAMSTEAD LOWER SCHOOL

1958	E M Rimes (from National School)
1965	Mr Purdy – Headmaster
1975	Mr A J Riley – Headmaster
1978	Mr King – Headmaster
1979	Maureen Pearce – Headmistress
1986	Mrs German – Headmistress
1986	Stephen Elphick –Headmaster

APPENDIX 3

Wesleyan Methodist Chapel Wilshamstead Sunday School Teachers 1826–1831

15th January 1826	**Superintendents**: William Armstrong Snr	
	Thomas Cooper	
	Daniel Harbour	
	Teachers: George Armstrong	Mary Dodson
	John Armstrong	William Green Jnr
	Thomas Armstrong	William Green
	William Armstrong Jnr	Mary Harbour
	Rebecca Bolston	George Litchfield
	Sarah Childs	Lovey Pearse
	Alice Cooper	Lydia Webb
	Keysia Cooper	William Whitemore
	Thomas Crowsley	Thomas Willmer
26th February 1826	Sophia Irons	Elizabeth Sharpe
7th May 1826	Joshua Armstrong	Elizabeth Tuffnail
	Hannah Spring	Sarah Tuffnail
	John Spring	
9th July 1826	George Armstrong Asst	Thomas Willmer Asst
	William Armstrong Jnr Asst	

3rd December 1826	Elizabeth Livett	Hannah Clark
10th February 1827	William Coles Joseph Cooper Mary Green	Benjamin Litchfield Elizabeth Scott
9th September 1827	Elizabeth Newman	
14th October 1827	Elizabeth Levitt Sarah Levitt Eleanor Roberts	Mary Toll William Toll
7th December 1828	Sarah Green William Pulley	Samuel Toll
1st March 1829	Elizabeth Toll	
7th March 1830	Samuel Barrick	William Mac Williams
19th December 1830	Elizabeth Scott	
6th March 1831	Thomas Toll Asst	
12th June 1831	Mary Ann Cooper Asst Mary Green	Susanah Irons Frederick Toll Asst
11th September 1831	Mary Ann Cooper	Frederic Toll
4th December 1831	William Coles	Elizabeth Dodson

APPENDIX 4

Wilshamstead and Westcotts Manors

WILSHAMSTEAD MANOR

Thought to be based at Manor Farm although the Lords of the Manor did not always live there.

1087	Countess Judith – Abbess of Elstow (1539 Abbey leased to Mr Holcrofte)
1539	Crown
1562	Robert Newdigate (conveyed in trust to John Newdigate)
1563	John Warner and Thomas Norwood
1565	Thomas Norwood (nephew of above)
1588	John Norwood
1605	Edmund Norwood
1608	Edmund Bagshawe and Francis Clerke

	Lady Elizabeth Radcliffe
1616	Thomas Hillersden
1628	Corporation of London (Edward Ditchfield as trustee)
	Henry Lord Mordaunt
1649	Elizabeth, Margaret and Anne Mordaunt
	John Manley
1669–1670	Thomas Beech
1671	William Bedell
	Newdegate family
	John Carteret, Earl of Granville, Viceroy of India
	Sir George Carteret
1764	Robert third Earl of Granville
	Henry Frederick Thynne (later Carteret)
	Carteret family including: John third Lord Carteret; Reverend Lord John Thynne; Mr A C Thynne; Francis John Thynne
1914	Sale of Haynes Park estate Manor remains with descendants of Reverend Lord John Thynne 2nd Marquess of Bath
2002	Believed to rest with either the current Marquess of Bath at Longleat Park or a close relative.

WESTCOTTS MANOR

Thought to be based at Cotton End Manor Farm although the Lords of the Manor did not always live there.

Pre 1087	Socmen
1087	Nigel D'Albini
	Albini family
	St Amand family
	Braybroke family
	Beauchamp family
1428	Elizabeth Beauchamp
	Crown
1483–1484	John de Grey
1609	Henry Lord Mordaunt
	Elizabeth, Margaret and Anne Mordaunt
	John Manley
1669–1670	William Bedell Thomas Beech
1741	Thomas Baker
	James Baker and John Eldridge
1800	Samuel Whitbread
2002	Remains with the current Samuel Whitbread who is also Lord Lieutenant of Bedfordshire

Subsidy Rolls

1309
Hundred De Redburn
Wylshamsted

Name	s.	d.	Name	s.	d.
Ricardo Laurence	2	1 3/4	Johanne le Swon		6 1/2
Willo Chapman	2	4 1/2	Johanne Liying		5 1/2
Waltero Le Swon	2	8 3/4	Roberot de Welye	2	8
Ricardo Pays		18 1/4	Johanne le Spenser	4	9 3/4
Matilda Lede		14 1/2	Willmo Schepherde	12	
Waltero de Kempston		19	Rogero Attewode	3	7 3/4
Ricardo Chalwenhull		18	Maltilda Darlinge	5	5 1/2
Waltero Ambesone		20	Thoma Godma'	2	6 1/2
Willmo Asselone		20	Roberto de Northende	5	0 3/4
Simone Attewode	2	3 1/2	Nicholao Kinge		23 1/2
Waltero Coue		12 3/4	Johanne Mody	3	4 1/2
Ricardo Liuerich	2	1 1/2	Willo de Northende	11 1/4	
Rogero Lomb		18	Ambilia Trays	2	6
Willmo Haringe		8 1/2	Johanne Attewode	2	2
Alexanbro Vhelwrithe		13	Is' Roger	22	
Schorte Jone		7	Johanne de Maynderbur'	4	8 3/4
Rogero Modi	2	1 1/2	Waltero Chapman	2	6 1/4
			Summa totius Villate	74	1

1332
Hundred De Redebournstoke
Villata De Wilsamstede

Name	s.	d.	Name	s.	d.
Johanne Lede	3	0	Richero Mode	2	0
Willo Horn	3	0	Willo Asselyne	5	0
Petronilla Pays	3	0	Rogero ate Wode	4	0
Johanne Heroun	4	0	Gregorio Salatiel	3	0
Waltero le fitz Johan	2	6	Nicholao Triuail	3	6
Johanne le fitz Water	4	0	Richero Godmar	5	0
Johanne le Kyng	4	0	Johanne ate Northende	3	0
Johanne atta Hul	3	6	Simone Godefrei		20 1/2
Johanne Norht	4	0	Richero ate Northende	3	10
Nicholao Pernel	3	0	Richero Derlying	2	5
Agneta de Maudenbun	4	0 1/2	Roberto Leverych		20
Simone Caleuhull		21 1/4	Simone Ryk		20 1/4
Johanne Norht	4	0	Henrico de Wylie Taxatore	2	0
Willo de Wylie		12	Willo Doget		12
Regero Lambe	2	4			

APPENDIX 6

Wilshamsteede Shipmoney – 1637

	l.	s.	d.
Sir Samuell Luke Knt.	0	6	8
Mr Risley [vicar]			
for his vicarage		17	0
for his temporall estate		3	8
John Warner	1	11	0
The Mannor	1	0	0
The parsonage	1	10	0
Berry Pastures	1	0	0
Nicholas Cawne		8	0
John Smyth		9	0
Thomas Bigg		5	4
John Cawne		3	4
William Loveledge		3	0
George Cloudes			8
Thomas Lawman		3	6
Henry Doggett		1	4
George Keyes		7	0
William Welch		10	3
Thomas Otredge		1	6
Peter Tayler		3	0
Thomas Hoddle		5	4
John Stratton		1	6
William Mawdlin		1	6
John Upton*		1	0
George Cawne		1	6
John Awstin		5	4
John Stoughton		1	5
John Bennett*		1	0
Thomas Harbert			8
John Smyth			8
George Dearemer		1	6
Richard Headlinge		13	4
William Springnell		4	1
Lawrence Helder*		2	0
Thomas Squire		9	6
Thomas Vincent*		6	8
John Bray	1	1	8
William Dearemer		2	6
William Palmer		3	0

	l.	s.	d.
John Warner, Sherman		2	6
Richard Favell		1	3
George Edwards		2	0
John Edwards*		1	0
John Negus		1	2
William Beech		10	0
John Tassell		1	0
Thomas Man		3	0
Mistress Hornes wood	1	1	0
Cotton End			
Sir Oliver Luke Knt.		5	0
John Manley	1	10	0
Mr Tayler, clerke		4	6
Mistress Mordants woods	1	1	0
John Warner jnr.		13	4
Thomas Warner	1	0	0
Edward Albon	1	0	0
Thomas Andrewes*		4	0
George Edwards		6	8
George Coote*		5	1
John Canfield		4	0
John Sheffield		15	10
David Jones*		7	0
John Cricke*		3	9
Edward Allen*		4	4
Henry Jones		3	4
Edmund Betts			8
George Thody		5	0
William Garrett		2	0
Medbury land		5	0
Monks field		7	0
William Burgen*			8
John Wattson		2	6
Francis Steven*		1	8
William Cawne		1	0
John Hedlinge		2	11
Widdowe Burgis		1	0
Mathew Hudson*		1	0
Richard Deare			8
Richard Woolhead			8

Sum 251. 10s. 11d.
*Names thus marked accur also in
arrears of payment

Arrears of payment

	l.	s.	d.		l.	s.	d.
John Upton		1	0	David Joanes		7	0
John Bennett		1	0	John Cricke		3	9
Lawrence Helder		2	0	Edward Allen		4	4
Thomas Vincent		6	8	William Burgen			8
John Edwards		1	0	Francis Stevens		1	8
Thomas Andrewes		4	0	Mathewe Hudson		1	0
George Coote		5	1	Richard Woolhead			8
				Wm Springnell		5	0

Sum 11.19s. 4d.

ACKNOWLEDGEMENTS

The authors would like to extend special thanks to Mr Darren Rhoden for all his help with photographs, initial formatting, the design and production of the supporting website, the maintenance of overworked PCs and an objective view.

Grateful thanks go to our enduring proof readers Julie Norton and Jutta Crane for their help in checking the first draft.

Especial thanks go to all those people listed below without whom this book would not be as interesting as it is.

living in the village (alphabetical order):

RICK BAXTER
HILDA BOURNE
SYLVIA BOWEN
JANET BROOKS
LANCE BURR
DOROTHY & JUNE COOPER
BRIAN, ALAN & TRACEY CROUCH
JOAN ELKINS
STEVE FENSOME
MARK GIBSON
PHILLIP GREEN
VIVIEN HAWKEY
BOB & JEAN HERBERT
ROGER HOPKINS
DOROTHY HOUGHTON
BARRY HUCKLE
NIGEL JACOBS

MIRIAM LANGFORD
ANNE LOWE
MICHAEL MASKELL
JIM, AUDREY & CATHY McCARTHY
RAY NETTLESHIP
JOHN NEWBURY
MARGARET PEARCE
DIANNE & JOHN POPE
ROSE SUMMERFIELD
VIOLET SUMMERFIELD
JACKIE & PETER TANSWELL
MALCOLM TERRY
RAY TERRY
MABEL TUFFNELL
MIKE WARNER
MICK WHITE
ENID WISSON

Other:

JIM ARMSTRONG (Canada) -
ALAN CHANCE (Bedford)
KEN GREEN (Greenfield)

IOLA NEWMAN (Stagsden)
Rev. FREDERICK PALMER

ADAM RAINE (Leicester)
MARY SCOTT (Cotton End)
STELLA TERRY nee
COOPER (Northants)

SANDRA WHITAKER (Bedford)

ALBION ARCHEOLOGY - MIKE LUKE
BEDFORD & RIVER IVEL DRAINAGE BOARD
BEDFORD ROTARY CLUB - MICHAEL ROGERS

BEDFORDSHIRE COUNTY COUNCIL - STEPHEN COLEMAN
BEDFORDSHIRE LIBRARY SERVICE
BEDFORDSHIRE AND LUTON ARCHIVES AND RECORDS SERVICE
BUXTON ONLINE
EMMANUEL COLLEGE CAMBRIDGE - JANET MORRIS
ENGLISH HERITAGE
HERITAGE TRUST ANCIENT ORDER OF FORESTERS
ROYAL ARMOURIES
SOUTH AUSTRALIAN GOVERNMENT
ST MARY'S CHURCH HENDON
ST ALBANS CATHEDRAL - NORMAN POWESLAND
WILSTEAD BRANCH WOMENS INSTITUTE
WILSHAMSTEAD LOWER SCHOOL
WILSHAMSTEAD HOMEWATCH NEWSLETTER